THE
TEARS OF A MAN
FLOW INWARD

THE
TEARS OF A MAN
FLOW INWARD

Growing Up in the
Civil War in Burundi

PACIFIQUE
IRANKUNDA

RANDOM HOUSE

NEW YORK

Published in the United States by Random House, an imprint
and division of Penguin Random House LLC, New York.

RANDOM HOUSE and the HOUSE colophon are registered
trademarks of Penguin Random House LLC.

LIBRARY OF CONGRESS CATALOGING-IN-PUBLICATION DATA
Names: Irankunda, Pacifique, author.
Title: The tears of a man flow inward: growing up in
the civil war in Burundi / Pacifique Irankunda.
Description: First edition. | New York: Random House, 2022. |
Includes bibliographical references.
Identifiers: LCCN 2021011222 (print) | LCCN 2021011223 (ebook) |
ISBN 9780812997644 (hardcover) | ISBN 9780812997651 (ebook)
Subjects: LCSH: Irankunda, Pacifique—Childhood and youth. |
Burundi—History—Civil War, 1993-2005—Personal narratives.
Classification: LCC DT450.863.I73 A3 2022 (print) |
LCC DT450.863.I73 (ebook) | DDC 967.572042092—dc23
LC record available at lccn.loc.gov/2021011222
LC ebook record available at lccn.loc.gov/2021011223

Printed in the United States of America on acid-free paper

randomhousebooks.com

2 4 6 8 9 7 5 3 1

First Edition

Title-page image: copyright © iStock.com / guenterguni

Book design by Victoria Wong

*For Maman Clémence and
my brother Asvelt*

"When I took my grandpa's cows to pasture,
in the land of sorghum to which we had fled,
I often found myself singing a sad and
soothing song. When I felt tears streaming
down, I wiped my eyes and repeated to myself
what I had heard the adults say:
that the tears of a man flow inward."

Contents

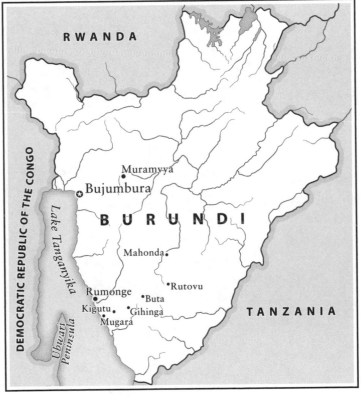

Prologue

A Country of Milk and Honey

"Time is a prison, and I sometimes feel
as if I am one of its inmates."

I find it hard to look back to Burundi, because I have always tried to look ahead. *Always*. Even as I think these words, looking out my window in Brooklyn, I realize I am nevertheless looking back.

I live in a spacious apartment, with six windows facing the water of New York Harbor. It is on the top floor of an apartment building so large it occupies the entire block between Shore Road and Narrows Avenue, next to the Verrazano Bridge. Below Shore Road lies the Belt Parkway. And below the Belt lies the Shore Promenade, and then the harbor, and across the harbor, Staten Island. I like to sit by my living room window, six feet wide, and gaze at the view. I gaze at it every day of the year, and not once have I tired of it.

When I lower my eyes, I look at a rose garden and water fountains and trees, and when I lift my eyes, I watch cruise and cargo ships pass by. These ships are enormous, and they come from all over the world—from Europe, Asia, Africa, Australia, and the Caribbean—bringing people and merchandise to New York. Local ferries and small boats and yachts go by faster than the great ships, which move slowly toward the harbor and slowly seaward toward the Narrows. Every cruise ship that passes grabs my attention. When there are no boats or ships out there, I find myself gazing long and longingly at a distant view. Instead of New York Harbor I see a view from the hilltop in Kigutu, my native village in Burundi.

I look out over Lake Tanganyika—the world's longest lake and second deepest—toward the peninsula of Ubwari, in the dark mountains of eastern Congo. I stare at the distant view and begin to journey back in thought. Then a cruise ship passes in front of me, grabs my attention, brings me back to Brooklyn, and makes me realize, as if awakened from a dream, that I was looking back. And I hear a voice stored somewhere in my mind, telling me not to look back.

It is the voice of my brother Honoré, telling me, as if I'd never heard it before, the story of Lot's wife, who looked back and turned into a pillar of salt. Hearing Honoré's voice in my mind takes me right back to Burundi, when I returned there during my winter break from Williams College. I still see the image of Honoré, standing in the yellow savanna grass dotted with small eucalyptus. He is telling me not to look back.

Years before, our mother, Maman Clémence, had given me the same advice more gently, saying to always look ahead. However, my older brother *drilled* "don't look back" into my psyche, so much so that it has disturbed me, causing a mixed effect: neither steadily looking ahead nor daring to fully look back, as if I have become a pillar of salt. Vladimir Nabokov wrote in *Speak, Memory* that time is a prison, and I sometimes feel as if I am one of its inmates.

I find it hard to look back because most of what I see when I look back is painful. One doctrine of Western psychology has long held that the cure for the pain of memory is a return to the past itself. Burundian culture holds an opposite view. I now realize that each approach has its own wisdom. But for me the past is inescapable.

In the late afternoon, the view from my window in Brooklyn brings me a feeling of peace, which reminds me of looking after cows. I liked to sit at the hilltop and watch the view of Lake Tanganyika while watching my family cows. I would gaze at the water in the lake and then gaze at the cows grazing.

I didn't know then that the cows of Burundi were unusual, because I didn't know that there were other kinds of cows. Ours were tall and long-legged and had enormous horns that could reach a span of ten feet from tip to tip, rising like cathedral arches above their peaceful-looking faces. They were called *inyambo,* and they were the most ancient of domesticated cattle, descendants of the biblical ox. Historians claim that these cows were present in the Nile Valley some four thousand years before historic times. Drawings of them were found on cave walls and ancient Egyptian monuments. *Inyambo* were known as the Cattle of Kings, although ordinary people owned them. One of my siblings had named himself Beninka, which means, literally, To Whom the Cows Belong; and my father was named Buhembe, the name of their long horns. Out of those long horns people made trumpets called *inzamba*. When I am asleep in Brooklyn, I sometimes hear a foghorn from departing cruise ships in New York Harbor; it makes a beautiful sound in the night, sad and distant, and it always makes me think of trumpets, of war, and of ancient times.

Like a person, my country had a name and a surname. If in bureaucratic American English I am "Irankunda, Pacifique," then my country is "Burundi, Milk and Honey." In the past, there had always been plenty of milk and excellent honey there. Beekeeping and the uses of honey had a place of importance in my country's traditions, and so did cows and their milk. As a child, I assumed this was my country's real name. Had I been asked, at that time, where I came from, I would have innocently said, "Milk and Honey."

That country no longer exists. It was the old Burundi, a country of storytellers, of people who invented myths and systems of justice and a set of traditions that had become folklore. Cows were a living relic of this old time, and in my family they were still treated and loved the way they had always been in the time of kings. Imana, God, was often referred to as "the creator of cows and children"—the two most adorable, precious gifts from Imana. When expressing shock or an exciting surprise, some Burundians invoked Imana, saying *Yampaye inka we*—"God who gave me cows!" In many ways, our cows were part of our family. Each new one was named at birth. Some were named after kings. It didn't matter that they were female. I remember we had a cow named

Mwambutsa, named for one of Burundi's kings, and every single one of her children and their descendants were also named Mwambutsa. We had another cow named Bwami, literally the Kingdom, and every one of her descendants was also named Bwami. Some of our family cows had names used in philosophical discourse—for instance, Jambo (the Word). Some had celestial names. I remember Juru (the Heavens), Zuba (the Sun), Gicu (the Sky), and Kwezi (the Moon). We had a very sweet-tempered cow named Buki—Honey. Other cows were named for their beauty, such as Kirezi—Pearl. She was indeed beautiful, but what impressed me most was her sense of fairness.

Pearl grew up an orphan. I remember my brother Asvelt telling me the story of how she lost her mother when she was still a baby and had to be nursed by another cow named Maza. Pearl eventually grew up and gave birth to her own baby. Around the same time, another cow named Ndava fell sick and couldn't nurse her calf. Pearl accepted this calf and nursed her as her own. At milking time, we'd let the calves out, one by one, and would escort each calf to the kraal where the mothers awaited. They were protective of their babies and would compete in lowing, and would push each other and even the calves of other cows, forcing their way to their own calves. But Pearl would *never* allow her own baby to touch her teat until her adopted calf arrived. She would kiss one and turn and kiss the other as she nursed them both.

I was fond of Pearl, but the cow I loved most was named Bigeni. When I was little, I would suck on her teat as if I were her calf. The milk was sweet and warm. I caressed her long neck, and she'd kiss my forehead and comb my hair with her tongue.

Although our cows were part of our family, bulls and aging cows could be sold away. I didn't know this as a child until, one morning, I heard my father say that he had sold Bigeni to our neighbors, who liked cows only for their meat and ate them as if a cow were just an impala! By evening I had plotted an escape. I whispered to Bigeni all the details. She and I were to embark the next morning to live in the forest where we would remain in daytime, hiding from the neighbors. I was scared of wild animals but Bigeni would protect me with her enormous horns. In the evening, we would come out. I would take her to graze in green pastures. I would feed her fresh grass and she would feed me fresh milk, and we would live together forever after.

By the time I woke up, the neighbors had arrived and taken Bigeni. I lay where she used to lie and cried all day long. We should have escaped in the night! I grieved over Bigeni for days. I often dreamed about her and I would wake up with my heart racing. Sometimes I dreamed I was living with her just as in the escape plan.

Looking back, those dreams seem prophetic. Soon after Bigeni was sold, the civil war broke out. It began in 1993 and lasted thirteen years. When it began, escape became my family's planning. During the years I was going to school, I took Maman Clémence's advice to heart: to always look ahead. The past meant struggles of family problems and a country falling apart in war. Present time was more of that. Looking forward was looking beyond past and present to whatever undefined thing lay ahead. But though I didn't realize it, looking ahead meant also carrying the deep past as my companion to the future.

For centuries, until the late 1800s, the king would send a delegation throughout the hills and villages of the country of milk and honey: they collected cattle and grain for the yearly eight days of our national festival. The cattle were brought to Muramvya and were led in a procession through the precincts of the royal court, wearing aromatic white flowers around their necks. Women followed the cattle, balancing tall baskets of sorghum flour on their heads. Fresh honey and an alcoholic drink made from fresh honey accompanied these offerings. Histories say that everything had to be of the best quality, even these baskets—you can see examples of those in the Metropolitan Museum of Art in New York.

The bulls in the procession were assembled on a hill for sacrificial offerings to God. Each bull was made to drink milk from the king's herd. There was a long process of selection before a bull was declared pure enough to become a burnt offering to Imana. The bulls that were not selected for sacrifice were eaten by the soothsayers. Legend has it that before a bull was slain, a soothsayer gently touched it three times with a magic wand called *ireba,* and the bull was immediately entranced, so that it remained calm and neither moved nor moaned even while being killed. There were precise instructions on how to dispose of the blood of the slain bulls and of their internal organs, which were thoroughly examined and washed, and then buried inside an enclosure called *urusha,* built with the trees of God.

The soothsayers prayed over the offerings to God in a small temple. When the signs showed that the offerings augured well—as they usually did, apparently—a joyful and prolonged voice called *impundu* resounded in the temple and beyond. Then the soothsayers invoked Nyange, the cattle egret and guardian of the ox, also known in Burundi as the bird of God and the king of birds. It has milky white wings and golden plumes. They also invoked God's other creations, including the hills, the views, and dawn, essentially invoking God, through God's creation, with a melodious chant of "May you have milk." Then the fathers and mothers placed their little children on mats woven from papyrus and gave the children milk in polished wooden pails made from flame trees. This was the time to present the first fruits of the harvest for the communion celebration called the Consumption of the Virgin.

The communion was followed by a silent nighttime procession. The following morning came the fresh-fire ritual. "The flame keeper" made the sacred fire using wood from the tree of God, and it was her duty to keep that flame burning throughout the year. It symbolized the eternal flame—an everlasting light. According to custom, everyone was supposed to extinguish the old fires in their houses and start every new year with a fresh one. The flame keeper used her sacred flame to light her neighbor's new flame, and that neighbor did the same thing for another neighbor. And so, it is said, fresh fire was passed from neighbor to neighbor, like gossip, throughout the kingdom of Burundi.

On the eighth day of the festival a horn was blown at dawn, and the soothsayers prayed for peace and prosperity in the kingdom. The ceremonies ended with a water rite called *gutota,* which was a sprinkling of the sacred water, using a leafy twig from the tree of God, to bless seeds and the cattle.

When I grew up, I was told of the festival, although not the details. I was also told that *inyambo* cattle, the Cattle of Kings, dwelt in the three old kingdoms of East Africa: Burundi, Rwanda, and Ankole, which is now the southwestern part of Uganda. My grandfather owned a large herd, more than 150, the largest herd in Mahonda (the land of sorghum), where he lived with three of his siblings who also had big herds but smaller than his. He had a field of tobacco, a substance he never smoked but only sold, in order to buy more *inyambo* cattle.

His wife, my grandmother, complained that he loved his cattle more than he loved her—and knowing her, I could well believe it. I heard stories of how he would decide to sell an aging cow and then would go into hiding, chagrined, when butchers came to take it away. When he heard the cow mooing, he would be consumed with guilt. One time he ran after the butchers, throwing their money at them and even offering more to buy back his beloved aged cow.

When I heard these stories, I wished my grandfather had been with me when my father sold Bigeni. Maybe he would have given me money to buy her back. Certainly he would have sympathized with my escape plan and would have understood my grief. When my grandfather died, my grandmother sold his cattle one by one until they were all gone. Afterward, the family herd contained only cows with medium-size horns—which, because of their puny horns, were considered a different species of cattle altogether. So in my grandfather's family, the Cattle of Kings disappeared at the hands of a small angry woman. Elsewhere in Burundi, war was mostly to blame.

THE
TEARS OF A MAN
FLOW INWARD

CHAPTER 1

The Beginnings of War

"Everywhere, desolation and tears."

I remember the day when the war began. It was in the middle of planting season. I was four years old. I was standing outside on the lawn in front of our house with my mother, Maman Clémence, and my brother Asvelt. A man who had been herding cows near our home came toward us. He was listening to a small radio he carried in his hands. "Where is he?" the man asked Maman Clémence, speaking of my father.

"He is not home," she said, reaching out her hand as they exchanged the greeting "*Amahoro*"—peace.

The man was a childhood friend of Maman Clémence, a Hutu from the same mountain village where she grew up. My parents were Tutsi, but before the war, especially in the countryside, this interethnic friendship was not uncommon. This old friend shook my mother's hand. He looked at her with a somber expression. "No, there is no peace," he said. Then he told her some terrible news. Burundi's recently elected president, the first democratically elected president and a Hutu, had been assassinated. The story had been aired on the BBC. The local radio station in Burundi had stopped broadcasting that day. Hutus in the country blamed the Tutsis. This was also true in our village, Kigutu. "They are very agitated," my mother's friend said of our Hutu neighbors. "Look for a place to hide."

Our Hutu neighbors had just destroyed a small Catholic church and smashed the drums inside. They had also destroyed two newly built houses that belonged to a Tutsi family. Maman's old friend had overheard some of our neighbors calling to others to remain vigilant so none of our family could escape. Maman Clémence started worrying aloud: "Where am I going to hide my children?" We wondered, *Would my father make it back home? Had he already been killed?*

For me and my family, this was the beginning of the thirteen years of civil war. My memories of the war's early years are truncated—mostly a collection of isolated events, memorable because they were traumatic and misremembered for the same reason. But I have assembled these memories as best I can. I have also relied on research and the memories of Asvelt and Maman Clémence.

Burundi's civil war began on October 21, 1993. It was an ethnic war, between the Hutus, who represent 85 percent of the population, and the Tutsis, who make up most of the rest. Generally speaking, it was waged over the grievances of Hutus against the Tutsis, who had ruled for most of the thirty years after Burundi's independence from Belgium in 1962. But I believe that the war's beginnings lay further back, with the Belgians' colonial policies. They occupied Burundi for forty years (following the German occupation), from 1916 to 1961, and during that time they excluded Hutus from the national administration. Most damaging of all, they destroyed Burundian traditions and institutions, including the Bashingantahe, the Institution of Wisdom.

The sparks of the war were unknown plotters in the Tutsi army who orchestrated the assassination of Burundi's president, Melchior Ndadaye. Because of his ethnicity, the Hutu radio station Milles Collines in Rwanda—soon to become the bullhorn of the genocide there—started calling on Hutus in Burundi to rise and avenge their assassinated leader. In only a few days, thousands of people were killed, mostly Tutsis, and mostly with machetes, by extremist Hutus. Soon afterward, the Tutsi army started hunting down the extremists who were committing the massacres, sometimes shooting indiscriminately and taking the lives of many innocent Hutus. Thousands of Hutus fled to Rwanda, Tanzania, and the Democratic Republic of Congo, and some of them formed militias that united against the Tutsi army. Collectively, these militias soon vastly outnumbered the army of the Burundi government, which, however, was better trained and had superior weapons. The two sides, the militias and the government army, began what would be a long fight, a brutal thirteen-year stalemate.

On December 6, 1993, two months after the assassination, President Ndadaye was buried along with some other murdered officials of his cabinet. There were a lot of Burundians at the funeral, and European ambassadors and expats. The Burundian archbishop, Joachim Ruhuna, presided at the funeral and read his sermon to the audience:

Dear brothers and sisters, Burundian men and women who listen to me, all of you, friends of Burundi:

. . . Look at the crime that is in front of our faces! Now the land of Burundi is littered with corpses, and soaked in the blood of our brothers and sisters. Yes, look everywhere. Let your gaze wander over the hills, and in the groves of banana plantations. You only see ash and rubble. Throughout the country, you hear weeping and wailing. You can no longer count widows and orphans. Everywhere, desolation and tears.

. . . Among the survivors, many are discouraged and fleeing . . .

The country is disfigured, pitiful. Those of us who are still here are afraid and ashamed . . .

. . . In the name of God and of the president deceased, whose corpse lies here before our eyes, I beg you to please stop the massacres and shed no more blood.

Our Burundi is so deeply wounded that it needs a president of great wisdom and full of humanity, who loves truth and justice, filled with great passion for the country and respected by all. For that president, we pray the Lord . . .

Another Hutu was appointed president and sworn into office. But he too was killed, along with Rwanda's Hutu president, Juvenal Habyarimana, when his airplane was shot down as it landed. Those killers also remain unidentified, though many theories per-

sist. That assassination happened in 1994, when Burundi's civil war was about six months old. In Rwanda,
the genocide of the Tutsis had been in the planning for
two years. Shooting down the plane was like the sig-
nal for the genocide in Rwanda to begin. The presi-
dents' deaths also intensified the civil war in Burundi.

When we heard the news of the assassination of
President Ndadaye, everyone at home was scared. "I
felt a different kind of fear than I had ever felt before," Asvelt told me later. What scared us the most
was to see adults scared. You felt shocked to realize
for the first time that your mom and dad could no
longer guarantee your protection, that they were just
as vulnerable as you were, that hardly anything was
predictable anymore, and that to trust anyone outside
the family was to be imprudent. Our world order had
been shattered. The life that had been jolly and play-
ful just yesterday suddenly showed me its dark side
and forced me at four years old to see life through a
Hobbesian lens for the next decade of war—a war
that made life nasty, brutish, and short.

After her childhood friend had told her the news
and warned her about our neighbors, Maman Clémence declared that we must leave the village. There
were four of us children still at home. "Collect your
clothes," she told us. We did as she said: we left the

house dressed in clean clothes, carrying bags on our backs. It was obvious to everyone we passed that we were leaving the village. All of the villagers except for three families were Hutu, and for some of them, our family and the two others in the village became their quarry. Some Hutu men cut a bunch of tree branches and made a blockade across the main path that led out of the village toward the mountains.

The local chief of this effort was named Fere, short for Frederick. The villagers called him Gorgo, but Fere had just declared himself *Shetani mukuru*—the great Satan. There must have been fifteen men standing in front of their barricade. They were brandishing spears and machetes. Other Hutu neighbors were passing by, men and women. Many of the women seemed to hide their eyes, as if embarrassed. But one of them shouted, speaking of us, "Don't let those tombs escape!" I didn't know that to call someone a *tomb* was an old insult, but it was frightening to hear someone speak as if we were already dead.

Gorgo and his men had stopped a Tutsi named Musa who had just fled to Kigutu from a nearby town called Mugara. He was lying on the ground, off to one side of the barricade, with several of Gorgo's gang standing over him. We heard Musa begging for mercy and offering to give the men his cows in exchange for his life, but they kept yelling at him. Meanwhile, my siblings and I stood facing the men at the barricade. One of them, a Hutu neighbor, stepped up to us and asked, with a menacing look, "Where is your father?"

We said he wasn't home.

"Did he go to bring soldiers?"

Before we could answer, the neighbor said, "Why did you kill Ndadaye?" He added, "Stay here. We will show you."

Another of Gorgo's men made a quick and sharp cut with his machete in the dirt road in front of us. Another looked into our eyes and, showing us his teeth, slid his index finger across his throat with one hand, holding a machete in the other. And then, one of the gang yelled at us, "Go back home!"

We ran back to our house. A few men followed us and camped in the road outside, evidently to make sure we didn't go anywhere.

We stayed inside the house that night, terrified. My father still hadn't returned. The next day Maman Clémence put our clean clothes in a filthy black container called *inkunguru* that is used to make palm oil and to soak cassava roots, and gave us new instructions. The four of us were to walk around the barricade. "If someone asks you where you are going, you say, 'We're going to dig cassava roots.'" It was early afternoon when we tried again to flee. The day was sunny but felt gloomy. We wore dirty clothes and carried farming tools and pretended we were just going to work on farmland nearby in the village. The men at the barricade were fooled. They let us pass.

We had a neighbor named Ananias and another one named Jeremiah. These two were the heads of the village's other Tutsi families, and they both had already managed to escape. Ananias lived at the far end of the village, on the path that led west toward the mountains, and Jeremiah lived on a hill right below the summit. Maman Clémence had told us, "Once you reach Ananias, you will leave the *inkunguru* there and put your clean clothes in black plastic bags. Then you will take a turn toward Kibimba and hike the hill to Jeremiah's house. Once you reach the summit, you will put on white clothes and make a brief stop, and I will know it's you."

I couldn't understand why Maman Clémence was staying behind. Perhaps it was explained to me that she was waiting for my father, but I didn't want to hear her say goodbye. I kept looking back as we walked, with my eyes tearing up.

When we reached the top of the hill above Jeremiah's house, we stopped and put on our white shirts and briefly gazed back to the village. I saw our house from there, way down on the plateau, and in the farther distance, the shining lake. Perhaps because I was little, it looked like our house was really far, very far away. At that moment I finally realized that Maman Clémence wasn't coming with us. "Let's go!" one of my siblings said. We continued among the mountains and walked for long hours, crisscrossing paths into villages, on hilly lands. During those miles and hours of walking, I felt tears rolling down my cheeks and a terrible anguish within. When we could no longer see home, I cried even more. At times I felt my legs giving way with exhaustion and then the rush of fear that made me forget my weariness and grief.

The vegetation in the mountains was different from that of the *imbo* plain—mostly woods of pine trees and eucalyptus, with open spaces of yellow savanna grass in between. As we walked on, I heard the wind whistle most of the afternoon. It stopped toward evening. We spent the night in a small, abandoned, thatch-roofed house by the road and walked on the next morning to my grandma's compound in Mahonda. I had calmed down by then. I was even eager to see my grandma's place. I had never been there before. It was bright and sunny that day, and I remember Asvelt pointing out Grandma's house to me: "It is that tin roof blazing with sun." In this mountainous region called *Mubututsi*—the region of the Tutsi—there was a large strong military base.

Some of my siblings were not home when the war broke out. One was in the capital, Bujumbura, in medical school, two were working, and three others were away at boarding school. And so we fled separately. Some of us stayed with relatives and others with host families, two fled abroad, and my parents remained in Kigutu.

The war went on for nearly fifteen years, but some parts of Burundi were safer than others. Soon after the war broke out, many military units were dispatched to various areas of the country that had been labeled Zone Rouge. My village of Kigutu was one of those, and a military platoon was later sent there.

After living with my grandmother for about a year, Asvelt and I decided to leave. We knew by then that she probably wouldn't notice we were gone, except when she had nasty chores she wanted done. We returned to Maman Clémence in Kigutu. We spent many nights there hiding in the forest from the Hutu militia who routinely passed through the village and occasionally came looking for us. To fool them, Maman Clémence made zigzagging paths in the grass. One went straight down the steep hill toward the valley. Another led to an open space and looked like it ended in gravelly land. We walked to our hideout on gravel, leaving no trace, right up to the entrance of our hideout inside the very tall *mukenke* grass. Sometimes when we were surprised by an attack and had to flee farther into the woods, we ended up sleeping without blankets on gravel. When the shooting quieted, we could fall asleep. At first it hurt to sleep on gravel, but you got used to it after a few times. We would wake up with aching backs and with gravel shapes marked on our skin like the indentations of fingers pressed into a ripe fruit.

It was painful when it rained on us. We couldn't sleep at all, especially when there was a storm. We spent the night shivering with cold, with no cover except our soaked clothes, beneath wet dripping trees or the *mukenke* grass where we hid. But even when it did not rain, we often woke up in the dawn feeling a cold and heavy dew falling on us from the leaves above.

When daylight came, we just resumed our daily routines, as if we were leading a normal life amid the abnormality of everything else. Once in a while, while farming, we saw the army's planes, which people called *kajugu-jugu,* crossing above our village and bombarding the mountains of Rukambasi, situated some twenty kilometers to the west of our village, where the militia had installed their main base. Nearly every week we heard heavy artillery and bombs going off in Rukambasi. It was during the night that the militia descended from those mountains into villages, often just to loot—because those villages were mostly Hutu populated—but sometimes also to kill, when Hutu civilians did not cooperate. There were types of guns that shot, during the night, burning bullets that people called *tracantes*—tracers. When they were fired, you saw the bullets flying like thin small flames and you heard a prolonged sound floating on the air.

For a long time during the war, many people stopped farming. A saying arose that seemed to summarize a general attitude: "Why grow food when I might not live to harvest it?" Many students were dropping out of school. But Maman Clémence had a great calm confidence in herself, and when she spoke to you, she spoke with the same confidence in you, as if she were in fact transferring her own confidence into you and you felt it penetrating. I often wondered what Asvelt and I would have become if it hadn't been for Maman Clémence. Everything else back then seemed designed to rob us of all hope—the war and all its evils, and our father's alcoholic ways. What really hurt me most about my father was his absence during the war. He was often somewhere far away from us, either literally away from home or drunk. And this was the time when we needed him most, for some sort of reassurance, for protection. Our neighbors in Kigutu terrified me. Even kids who had been classmates of my older siblings turned against us once the war began.

I remember one boy named Mworora, a classmate of one of my siblings. He led a group of boys to our house to steal our goats. Each carried a machete. But luckily, that day my father was home and sober, and when he confronted them, the boys ran away. Right now, as I write, Mworora is a grown man, recently in the news from Burundi—infamous for killing political dissidents. While my family and neighbors in Kigutu knew the kid as Mworora, today the rest of Burundi knows him as Rwembe—the Razor. Some of the boys in my village who joined the militia repeatedly returned to hunt my family and some of our neighbors. Once in a while, I really did wonder if there was any point in enduring the pain and risk of going to school. But just as she encouraged us to keep on farming, Maman Clémence insisted that we keep going to school. Looking back, it seems to me that Maman Clémence had decided to become a commandant in another type of war, and Asvelt and I became her troops.

. . .

The war had seasons for me and my family. There were times when four Hutu rebels who were natives of Kigutu brought their militias to the village nearly every week, and times when our Hutu neighbors would gather at the village's earthen mound, a traditional place of assembly, and preach ethnic hatred, sessions that sometimes turned into drinking bouts. And there were times when units of the Tutsi government army camped in the village and the militiamen stayed away. And then there were times when no soldiers of either side were around. These were periods of relative peace even for us—most neighbors no longer dared to threaten us, for fear that government soldiers would find out and take revenge.

During the thirteen years of war, we lived in perpetual fear and in danger of violent death. But during the times when war quieted, we stayed home and slept in our house, which allowed us to focus on school and to help Maman Clémence with farming. Though drunk nearly every evening, when he was home my father took care of the cows and ran a palm oil business. He didn't make the palm oil himself; he rented out the plantations. One time, Asvelt and I paid a young man named Gasongo to help us plant—at my father's request—about ten more acres of palm trees. We planted them close to home in the valley of the river Gasagamba. Once the palm trees grew, Asvelt and I stood up to our father and refused to let him rent them out. Asvelt and I made the palm oil ourselves and sold it to support Maman Clémence. It was an intense kind of labor to make palm oil, but we always paid one or two people to help us, and we only worked there on weekends and when we were on vacation from school. We processed the nuts in a palm oil mill called *intigisi,* which was installed by the river. It worked like a turnstile and was man-powered. The shafts made four angles. Three or four people stood in each angle between two shafts. You pushed one shaft to the front with one arm and pulled the other shaft from behind with your other arm, and you went around and around for about three hours. To rest your arms, you usually switched, so that the arm that had been pulling was pushing, and vice versa. The oil dripped into a large pan and was channeled into a pipe that led through the ground into a large hole. The soil was clay and made a solid container. After the oil was sucked out of the nuts' outer shells, we ground what remained and sold them to a factory that turned them into soap. The whole process was tedious and tiring, but profitable.

What we really enjoyed was farming. Maman Clémence, Asvelt, and I tilled a lot of land and grew beans, corn, sweet potatoes, taros, plantains, mountain rice, and cassava roots. We made small gardens for tomatoes, eggplants, pineapples, cabbages, pumpkins, and a green vegetable with spear-shaped leaves called *lenga-lenga*. Of the food we grew, only mountain rice was a bit tiresome, especially weeding and harvesting. But we liked eating rice. There was even a song that kids usually sang while preparing rice. To remove the husks, we pounded the grains using a mortar called *isekuro* and a pestle. While pounding, you heard kids singing with the rhythm of the pestle's pounding: *Sekura mudidizo, nawurimye bambona*— "Pound, pestle, pound. Pound the rice I grew." And kids went on improvising other verses. We had several orange, guava, and avocado trees, one mango tree, and some blackberry bushes and passion fruit called *imarakuja*. We also had chickens, goats, sheep, and of course we raised the long-horned *inyambo* cows. The goats and sheep we sold, and we ate the chickens and eggs but never the cows.

When school resumed, we tried to help Maman Clémence in the mornings and evenings and on weekends. Our elementary school was about six kilometers from home. And oftentimes we ran the whole way to school to avoid being late, and back from school so we could help Maman Clémence before dark. Altogether it was a lot of work, but you always had a great feeling of satisfaction. And we had a great coach in Maman Clémence.

She believed that good work started early. Her alarm clock was the crowing of a rooster. Before six in the morning, she would wake us up, saying: "The rooster has already crowed. Wake up, my dear." We had abundant harvests every season, which she often shared with some of our neighbors who didn't have much land.

Maman Clémence had never gone to school, but she was determined that we would. When we first started school, she explained education to us with farming metaphors so that we felt as though at school we were just going to continue doing what we did with her at home. A pen was now your hoe, she said, and she saw to it that we had notebooks and all the other tools we needed for school. As for intelligence, Imana gave you a brain. What you needed to do was to apply diligence to your studies. Then you would harvest knowledge. She seemed to want to convince us that teachers are like parents. You should be polite and listen attentively. If you carry yourself in ways that are not right, or if you don't do well, the teachers will be really sad. See, they talk to you for hours and hours, for days and days on end. Imagine if you tilled land and worked your farm all year long, and at the end you harvested nothing. After saying all this, she wished us a good harvest.

I was very quiet at school, and I never played with other kids. Teachers organized dancing lessons, but I boycotted them. To me, life was not nice, and I was not going to dance for it. Life was unforgiving and I was not going to play with it. While other kids would be playing on their way back from school, Asvelt and I hurried home to help Maman Clémence with chores.

Some of the home chores that Asvelt and I did, such as sweeping the house and the yard, cooking, carrying baskets on our heads, and washing Maman Clémence's clothes, were seen as "ladies' work." When our neighbors saw Asvelt and me doing these chores, they seemed amused. We were used to being teased, often by ladies, but in a friendly way. Once I heard a woman teasing Maman Clémence, saying, "I see you've got girls to help you." Our neighbors might have thought that Maman Clémence made us do these chores against our will. There was, for instance, a Burundian tradition called *kugemura*, in which women balanced tall baskets on their heads that were filled with presents and included crops like peas, rice, flour, fruits, other kinds of food, and gifts. This happened usually when a person paid a visit to a relative or friend after a long absence or when there was an event or a ceremony. Traditionally boys never carried these baskets. But because Maman Clémence had become frail and suffered recurrent migraines, Asvelt and I accompanied her and carried the baskets, which drew all eyes to us.

Maman Clémence had a cow named Kiyago who wouldn't let anyone else milk her. One time when Maman Clémence was sick, Asvelt put on some of her clothes and went to milk that cow. People saw Asvelt and laughed at him, but he didn't care and neither did the cow, who was fooled and didn't try to kick him.

What Maman Clémence sometimes made us do against our will was take milk to an elderly lady named Zera every morning before we went to school. Asvelt and I had nothing against Zera. In fact we really liked her. We called her Bibi—a Swahili term for grandma. Her family, however, seemed to want to give us all possible reasons to despise them. Zera was a Hutu. Before the civil war, we had been getting along with her family just fine. But when the war broke out, one of her sons became a member of Gorgo's gang—the men who had blocked our way when we had first tried to flee Kigutu. He and Zera's other sons often sneered and spat at us when we passed by, for no apparent reason, even when we were bringing milk to their mother. When there was a child in the village who got sick, our neighbors always came to my family to ask for milk, and they knew that Maman Clémence would give it to them for free. And yet Zera's family and some other neighbors were not shy about telling us that cows from a Tutsi family were not welcome to graze on their land. When Zera's sons told Asvelt and me to take our cows off their land and we knew that we had to bring milk to their mother the next morning, we wanted to rebel against Maman Clémence. But she would remind us that while what they did was wrong, it was not Zera who had done it. Maman Clémence seemed to have taken a position of her own, and she always acted in a kind and respectful way even when the other person behaved otherwise. The way she dealt with our grandmother Musaniwabo was especially frustrating. We wanted nothing to do with the old harridan, but Maman Clémence would not allow us to talk ill of her. "It is sad that she does not show you affection, but you should show her love. She is your grandmother!" To pay respect was not optional. We had to be polite to everybody, including our nasty grandmother. Maman Clémence talked to us about love as if it were an organ like every other of our organs but the vital one without which our humanness was essentially dead. "If you have no love, you're nobody," she liked to say.

Maman Clémence elevated people in a subtle but effective way. Whenever you indulged in negative talk about someone who had wronged you, showing resentment and expecting her to sympathize and take your side, you realized that she not only believed that your resentments were wrong but they were also repugnant, something to be looked down upon. She would try to make you realize that speaking this way was beneath you. She would tell you this with a gentle tone that calmed you and made you ready to listen to her advice. In Burundi, there is a whole euphemistic language and vocabulary for gentle communication called *imvugo mbabarira matwi,* literally a "feel-sorry-for-the-ear manner of talking." This was how Maman Clémence talked to and calmed us. If you still burned with anger, there was a sharp sentence she liked to use, which always got our attention: "You see, my child, listen to me, a person shouldn't milk a dog and another person respond by forcing that same milk into the first person's mouth. Are you with me?" Any Burundian would have understood this. To milk a cow was a dignified act, but to milk a dog would be a perversion, so foul indeed as to turn the milker into a virtual dog. But it was just as bad to try to punish the act by forcing the real dog's milk into another human being's mouth. That is, as she would explain again, if people did things to you that offended human dignity, you must not lower yourself by doing the same sort of thing back. She would say this as if in passing. Then she would emphasize the things you *should* do. She rarely talked about the things you shouldn't do. It was as if she were trying to distract you from thinking about negative things by encouraging you to focus on doing positive things. You couldn't escape the reality that surrounded you, of course, but the way I understood her advice was that you could always choose what to focus on.

The Bashingantahe

"I will always serve the cause of truth."

In the old kingdom of Burundi, it used to be that every village had certain people who were universally known to be wise and just. They lived among their neighbors in the hills and mountains, and in the large settlements of Burundi. These were ordinary people, farmers and cow herders, but you could not become one of them unless *everyone* in your village agreed that you were wise and just.

Then you had to be trained. These chosen people advised and settled disputes at every level from the village to the king's court, and according to the histories everyone trusted and respected their judgment, including the king. As a group, they had so much power that they had both the right and the responsibility to tell the king, when he was harming the kingdom, that it was time for him to "give himself honey"—that is, to drink honey laced with deadly poison.

They were called the Bashingantahe (pronounced ba-*shingan*-high). In Kirundi—an old and rich and very complex language—there are many composite words, and Bashingantahe is one. *Shinga* in this case means "to decide." And *ntahe* embodies the concepts of justice, order, and equity. These are supposedly incarnate in a rod called a baton of justice, cut from either of the two species called the trees of God. *Ba* is a prefix that signifies "many," and *mu* means "an individual." Thus Bashingantahe means "many wise and just people," and a Mushingantahe (pronounced moo-*shingan*-high) is simply one of them. Burundi's old monotheistic religion incorporated into its teachings the importance of these just and wise people.

This judicial institution, perhaps unique in the world, seems to have been organized in the 1500s, around the same time as the monarchy. Three legends narrate the origin. In the most fanciful, Death and a creature called Monster are having a fierce argument. (Monster, a familiar figure of Burundian fables, is part human and part animal.) Death says, "I own people, I can kill whomever I want." Monster replies, "That's not true! You are a killer like any other killer. The one who owns people is God, He who creates. When ten die, a hundred are born. When a hundred die, a thousand are born. And so how do you own people?" In the midst of this dispute a renowned wise man called Sacega happens to walk by and mediates the dispute between Death and Monster, even though he knows that he will be killed for performing this duty. Sure enough, when he finds against Death, declaring that God is greater, Death bites him in the neck. Hearing the story, the king in effect makes wisdom into a formal institution. He declares to Sacega's followers: "Mushingantahe, you shall not fear. Abide by justice and die for it if you have to." In the fable, the king then directs the assembled Bashingantahe to build a courthouse, and to name it *sentare,* literally "father of the lion"—father, that is, of the king of the forest. It used to be taught in the folklore that giving the court this name amounted to a proclamation that the laws of justice ruled over the laws of the jungle.

Some Burundian historians and anthropologists wrote about the institution of Bashingantahe in Kirundi and in French. All their accounts offer nearly identical descriptions of the several years of arduous training that candidates underwent and of the final ceremony that was held for those who passed it. The ceremony was performed all over the country, usually at a village's meeting place—typically, an earthen mound with a small building beside it, where the Bashingantahe of the village would meet with citizens to resolve the town's problems. The candidate's family and most of the village would attend the induction ceremonies.

The audience would sit below the mound. The celebrants were positioned on top of it. The candidate would rise and the Mushingantahe in charge would ask him a series of questions, including these: "Do you agree to obey the laws of the country, to be merciful and serve the unfortunate?" "Do you agree to be the light of the country, to do justice without bias and to avoid corruption?" "Do you agree that you will raise your children with these values?" The candidate having answered yes to all the questions, the Mushingantahe in charge would ask him to repeat this oath: "I agree, and I swear to the king and to the Bashingantahe, that I will always serve the cause of truth in the conflicts that I will have to arbitrate." Then the candidate's mentor, a Mushingantahe himself, would come forward and speak these words (the translation is mine):

> I lay the baton of justice [*intahe*] in your hands. According to the customs of Burundi, I give it to you in the name of the Bashingantahe of this country because you fulfill all the conditions required of every person of truth. If you used to lie, you must renounce lying. We consecrate you in broad daylight before the world.

From this day on, if you pass by a place where there are conflicts, you must resolve them. You have just received *intahe*. Know that you are no longer a child. When you are insulted, you will not reply with insults. In your mouth, there will always be words of truth and you will always follow the laws that will move this country forward. Be wise and do not be afraid of telling the truth, even when you must die for it. Those who have died for the truth are still praised today. We hold their graves in high esteem. You will always take this country to your heart. You will fight for the orphans. You will be the solace for the lonely. Be brave by giving yourself to the poor. It is under this condition that God will watch over you. Know now that you should represent God and the king. Be discerning. Be prudent. You have just reached a milestone. In this work, you will not seek riches. You will be the right path in whom this country will trust. You become the pillar on which the unfortunate will lean. You will be the granary of peace. You will be a joy for the king and the Bashingantahe.

The mentor would give the candidate a chair and say: "Take this seat. It is a sign that you have become a Mushingantahe. You will use it to provide justice. Be respected by the young and the old. Seated here, you will be in the place of God."

Down below, the audience would clap their hands and cheer for the new Mushingantahe and sing *impundu*—a prolonged sound of praise. After the cheering, the mentor would conclude the ceremony, saying to the candidate: "I have now finished my role. You have heard the responsibilities that you will assume. May God bless you and may you serve Burundi by showing what you as a Mushingantahe now have in greater abundance than others."

I first saw the description of this ceremony four years after I arrived in the United States. It seemed like what I had been praying for since the middle of Burundi's civil war.

CHAPTER 2

Maman Clémence

"Make me a Mushingantahe,
like Maman Clémence."

In Burundi, it used to be that elders greeted little children with a blessing. When I was little, I remember being confused by their wishes. Like a priest blessing a newly baptized baby, they put the palm of their hand on your head and wished you *Gira so, Gira inka, Gira izina, Gira iyuva, Gira iyuja, Gira ibibondo:*

May you have a father.
May you have cows.
May you have a name.
May you have an origin.
May you have a purpose.
May you have children.

Some greeted you only with the first three wishes. Some went on and greeted you with all six. I believe most children understood these words simply as a greeting, just as adults in Burundi say "Amahoro"—peace—to say hello. Even though I never questioned the elders' list of wishes, I do remember wondering about them. Of the six, only one made sense to me then: *Gira inka*—May you have cows. But "May you have children"? I was a kid myself, why would I care about having children? "May you have a name?" I already had one—Ira, my childhood name. "May you have an origin?" or "May you have a purpose?" Everyone, even adults, needed to think about those. What in the world could these wishes mean to a little one? "May you have a father?" When the elders found me at home with my father and greeted me with this blessing it made me want to say, "Don't you see him?"

But to me, the strangest thing about those wishes was that they did not include mothers. Imana had certainly blessed me with mine: Maman Clémence. She often told me about her parents, and she spoke fondly of them. Alas, I never met them. By the time she bore me, both had died. But unlike me, she lived a happy childhood. What little she knew about misery, she said, came from a man playing a flute, a sorrowful lone man who lived on a hill near her parents' house. It seemed as if the only sadness she remembered about her childhood was this man's flute blues. While looking after calves, in early morning or late afternoon, she used to hear him playing and then singing these mysterious words: *"Mukobwa utaragogwa, uraza undabe, niwamara kugogwa uzoba nkanje"*:

Lady who has known no misery, come see me.
Once you experience misery, you will be
    like me.

She did not go to see the lone man. She never knew what had happened to him. Later, when she was married, the bleak prophecy came true for her, her family, and her country. And for the first time she experienced both the miseries of family trials and the tribulations of war. But these miseries didn't turn Maman Clémence into a miserable lady. Instead they brought out the best in her, an embodiment of my country's old traditions of wisdom.

Maman Clémence grew up in a place called Gihinga, a village set among beautiful mountains covered with pine and eucalyptus trees. Below there were prairies used for farming and grazing. There was a river in the valley where cows went to drink. And there were several fountains from which people fetched clean water. My mother's parents named her Mpozenzi, which means "I keep quiet though I know." And she was christened Clémence, "merciful" in French, in the Catholic church.

Maman Clémence's family and my father's were all mountain people. As children, she and my father went to the same Sunday Mass at the Catholic church in a place called Ndagano. But they didn't know each other until late in their youth. When my father began courting Maman Clémence, he had just started a small business as a salesman. He mostly sold men's suits in a town called Bururi and in another town called Kiremba, and he also sold and imported women's clothing and blankets from Tanzania. Recalling the early conversations she had with him in their courtship, Maman Clémence described my father as a calm but ambitious young man with many projects in mind. Soon after they were married, however, my father's hopes and ambitions began to drown in alcohol—drinking down the troubles that his mother brought upon him.

It all started with jealousy. My father had built his house right next to his parents', in the same family enclosure. And so Maman Clémence essentially lived with her in-laws and shared the same fence. When my father imported women's clothing from Tanzania, he would pick the nicest clothes for Maman Clémence. But every time my father did this, my Grandma Musaniwabo wouldn't talk to Maman Clémence for days. "These would have sold for a lot of money," she would grumble. "Look at this waste." Musaniwabo started telling her son that he was working himself too hard for his wife, that he didn't even have the time to be a gentleman and use the money he was making to go out and be with others. Musaniwabo soon made it unpleasant enough for my father not to want to spend time at home anymore. He started going to the bar nearly every evening. Most of the money he made ended up there.

All the children now depended on Maman Clémence alone: for food, clothing, and school, and care when they got sick. One time, two of my older siblings both fell sick at once and had to be hospitalized. When they recovered, Maman Clémence brought them home. But when she arrived, she found my sister and my brother Asvelt very sick and had to go back to the hospital with them the same day—a walk of about twenty kilometers. She carried my sister on her shoulder. And she carried Asvelt on her back and carried me in her womb. And carried the burden of all this in her mind. My sister was about four years old. Asvelt was about a year and a half. And she was, she guessed, about five months pregnant with me. When she arrived back at the hospital, laden with children, a lady married to a wealthy man named Bikota told Maman Clémence, speaking of me, "You will not be able to raise this one." She advised an abortion, offering to pay for it and adding this reassurance: "Nobody will know, it will be done with dignity." Maman Clémence rejected the offer. She carried her pregnancy to full term, and I was born. I was her last, the ninth.

Day after day, her struggles kept mounting, and the troubles her mother-in-law caused seemed endless. To get away from Musaniwabo, my parents moved to an uninhabited hilltop called Mpete, but it was only about three miles away—not far enough from Musaniwabo. The troubles went on, and my father kept drinking.

Finally, my parents moved a lot farther, to the region called *imbo,* in the lowlands. The plains of *imbo* stretch toward Tanzania in the east and to the mountains of the Congo-Nile divide in the west. My parents settled above the plains, in a village called Kigutu, and built their house on a plateau facing Lake Tanganyika. Around the plateau there were undulating mountains descending and plunging into the waters of Tanganyika. For mountain people, the *imbo* region was a land of economic opportunity: palm oil plantations, fertile farms, and the lake's fecund waters for fishing. Men in the mountains were admired at home for working in *imbo* but were looked down upon for raising their families in that palm oil region. Mountain people often said that people in *imbo* were uncultured and ill-mannered, among other things. My mother was reluctant to move there but my grandfather, Musaniwabo's husband, understood my mother's pain, and though sad to lose her, he encouraged her to go, believing that things would improve for her if she moved away from Musaniwabo. And after my family moved, things did improve for Maman Clémence.

Back then, land was cheap in Kigutu. Cows were more valuable. My father sold several cows that Maman Clémence had inherited from her family and used the money not on alcohol for once, but to buy land on Kigutu's plateau and in the valley below. He also bought several palm oil plantations: one in a place called Mambi, another in a place called Kigwena, and another in a place called Karonda, alongside Lake Tanganyika. We lived in a fairly big house, with brick walls and a tin roof. It had six bedrooms and two common rooms for sitting and dining, and an outhouse.

. . .

Sometimes other people's memories become more vivid to you than your own. Asvelt told me a story about Maman Clémence that I didn't witness, but it is one of the most vivid memories I have of her.

We had left Kigutu for a while, as we sometimes did when the war heated up. We had fled to a place called Kabwayi. There was a military station there, and there were many refugees, both Tutsis and Hutus, people like us who had fled their villages and installed their tents near the army barracks. The self-appointed ruler of this refugee settlement was a soldier named Minani. He and his subaltern were almost always together, and everyone feared them. They talked only to each other, and to everyone else they gave commands. They liked to walk with sticks, which they used to beat up people, including their own soldiers. I remember one soldier who was play-wrestling with his friend, and when Minani caught them by surprise, he picked one of the two and ordered him to do push-ups while Minani beat him with his stick: two beatings per push-up, one on the way down, another on the way up. The soldier sweated over dozens of push-ups to the rhythm of the beating.

Minani and his comrade often wore serious and even menacing looks. They talked in an odd dialogue, one word at a time, with a considerable interval between the words. When they walked by you, they never said hello. And nobody dared to say hello to them. But many of the other soldiers were friendly to us civilians. Some were even mischievous and played with kids. When Minani and his comrade returned to the barracks from their walk, you saw soldiers arranging themselves and quieting. It was truly frightening when Minani and his comrade caught a Hutu militiaman. They would torture him in public when everyone was watching.

One time they caught a Hutu civilian from a place called Bukanda, a man accused of inciting his Hutu neighbors to join the militia. They tied up the man and put him in a gutter by the road and beat him with sticks while rainwater ran over his body. A big crowd gathered, watching in silence. Asvelt found himself in the crowd watching too. The mayor of commune Vyanda happened to be visiting refugees that day, and when he passed by, he stopped and had a brief conversation with Minani. But to Asvelt's surprise, nothing changed. The militiaman lay in the gutter and as the mayor left, Minani and his colleague went back to beating him.

And then in the midst of all this, Asvelt saw Maman

Clémence appear on the top of the hill above the road. She had come from Kigutu, bringing us food. When Asvelt saw her, he felt nervous and scared. He was sure Maman Clémence would try to get the soldiers to stop torturing this man. How would Minani and his comrade react? His first instinct was to go meet Maman Clémence and somehow distract her. There was a path parallel to the road. Maybe he could lead her to this path and avoid the road. He started walking fast toward her. Then Minani and his comrade noticed Maman Clémence, and Asvelt heard them say hurriedly to their soldiers: "Get him out! Get him out!" And then Minani and his comrade slowly walked away from the man and in the direction of Maman Clémence, as if they were simply patrolling the village, pretending nothing was happening.

When she reached the soldiers, Maman Clémence greeted them: "How are you, *bane*?" (The word *bane* literally means "children," but it is also used as a word of endearment—when used by someone your parents' age.) The soldiers called her Maman and responded politely that they were fine, and asked her about the security situation in Kigutu. For the first time, Asvelt said, he realized that Minani and his comrade were capable of respecting someone. There had been consistency in their intimidating behavior, but now they were the ones who seemed to bow. The crowd noticed.

Asvelt said nothing to Maman Clémence. She hadn't noticed what had just happened. He was relieved but also puzzled. Why would the village martinets hide the incident from Maman Clémence when they didn't even hide it from the mayor—they who intimidated everyone? Why was it that they were afraid of Maman Clémence—they who seemed to respect no one? What was it about her?

The fact that just one individual's appearance in a large crowd could change the atmosphere entirely seems to me like evidence that there was something about Maman Clémence, something greater than the power that Minani and his comrade wielded over everyone else in Kabwayi. In retrospect, I think it was the fact that she did not see them as soldiers but as other children, and that she held them to the same standards that she expected her own children to meet. Maman Clémence showed them respect and tender love. These were things she seemed to have completely internalized. When she saw soldiers mistreating somebody, she talked to them as if she were talking to her own children. I think they were surprised that she confronted them when everyone else feared them. She didn't do this in a hostile or argumentative way. It was as if she were disappointed and surprised by what they were doing, as if she were their mother and they knew what she expected of them. The way she talked to them was not talking down but lifting them up. She was telling them in effect that what they did had to be a mistake. Otherwise they would not have acted in a manner that was, in her eyes, inhumane. It seemed as if she had her own good image of them and wondered, *How come you just made such a terrible mistake?* For them, I think this mistake had been normalized and integrated into their way of behaving. People around them expected this behavior—and this encouraged it. But for these soldiers to be told by someone who seemed to care for them that what they were doing was wrong and out of character was, I think, a compliment to them, and uplifting. And I believe that's why even Minani and his colleague wanted to hide the truth from her whenever they made what she would call "a terrible mistake."

When my father died, his last words to my mother were a sad self-reflection of a defeated husband and regretful father: "I have not lived well by you," he said to Maman Clémence. "But you became a Mushinga-ntahe. What saddens me the most is that our children might model themselves after me, and if they do, I am leaving you no children. But remain a Mushingantahe and look after the younger ones."

As an adult now, I have come to make some sense of my elders' greetings to little ones. I understand that "May you have an origin" and "May you have a purpose" are indeed blessings. And if I were to bless my little country the way my elders blessed little children, I would wish Burundi to be known in the world for its old Institution of Wisdom: the Bashingantahe. And if I were to say a prayer in the manner of Saint Francis of Assisi, I would pray, "Lord, make me an instrument of your peace. Make me a Mushingantahe, like Maman Clémence."

CHAPTER 3

The Old Kingdom

"I find myself thinking that civil war would
have been nearly impossible in Burundi
when the Bashingantahe still lived."

The old kingdom of Burundi was fiercely indepen-
dent. In the late 1800s, Arab slave merchants
roamed black sub-Saharan Africa. One European witness wrote: "The cruelty of their methods of warfare
paralyzed the whole population with terror." But
those methods failed in Burundi. The same European
wrote:

The Rumalisa slave merchant of sinister reputation
reached the northern tip of Tanganyika with his
guerrilla band Wangwana. But then they ventured,
equipped with their firearms, and crossed into Burundi to capture slaves. King Mwezi Gisabo lured
the Arabs into the interior of Burundi and almost
completely annihilated them. The impression made

on Arabs was such that they never dared again to rub up against Burundians.

Burundi's king commanded a well-organized and disciplined army. But it was no match for the modern weapons of the Germans, who first arrived in 1884, intent on turning Burundi into a tame little colony. A German anthropologist who had surveyed Burundi for his country's colonial project had written something like a warning: "Burundians are a peaceful people if you leave them in peace." He had added: "They are difficult to engage because they have a strong sense of independence and an acute sense of freedom, and their spirit is fully awake. That is why it will be years before the German government can establish a true administration in Burundi, as simple as it is."

The king resisted for nearly twenty years, finally surrendering and signing a treaty on June 6, 1903. But revolts kept breaking out even after the treaty, and when they did, the German response was extremely violent. The Germans, misunderstanding Burundi's culture and political structure, imagined that the country's Hutu were a docile, simpleminded majority, and that the Tutsi controlled everything and were therefore the main obstacle to the colonial enterprise, including Christianization. Accordingly, the German authorities began targeting the Tutsi.

The German military expeditions in Burundi are best documented by Roger Botte in "Rwanda and Burundi, 1889–1930: A Chronology of a Slow Assassination." From 1896 to 1914, some forty-eight military expeditions were launched throughout the country, and in nearly every one of them cows were shot or confiscated—on some occasions, thousands of cows—and cows were central to Burundi's economy and culture. This account of a German raid is typical: "killed quite a number of people, especially women and children; burnt the entire country; took 1,500 cows . . . hung two princes."

In most of the raids, the murder and theft of cows and the burning of crops amounted to a calculated attempt to cause famine, which the Germans called "a necessary and inevitable outcome of war." One German wrote in praise of this strategy: "Their cows will die, famine will come, sickness will finish off those whom famine will have left upright." By 1914, fifteen outbreaks of famine had occurred in various parts of the country, including famines caused by disease.

The German invasion of Burundi contained many absurdities. For one thing, there was the disproportionate power of the weapons they used. (It has been said that the Germans used Burundi as a site for testing some of the machine guns they employed in World War I.) There was the Germans' apparent fondness for the place they were setting ablaze, the satisfaction with which they admitted their atrocities, the meticulousness with which they recorded them, and the sentiment some colonists professed for the people they murdered. Here is a German colonist describing his feelings toward the Tutsi who were being slaughtered:

> If I honestly want to analyze and define my feelings, I have to say frankly that they impressed me. To this day, I have not been able to get rid of this feeling, even if my reason resists it. . . . I evidently asked myself questions about the root causes of this singular sentiment toward colored people. . . . There is their gigantic stature, the nobility of each of their movements, the dignity with which they express themselves, their way of dressing discreetly and with taste, their distinguished features, their calm and penetrating gaze . . . and on top of all this, there is—but here I'm whacked, I cannot give a shape to what I perceive in a manner that is obscure and foggy.

One German businessman described what his countrymen were doing as "periodic butcheries." The historian Roger Botte describes one of those, a fairly typical German military raid, which occurred in 1908:

> From 31 March to 18 May, Grawert leads a new expedition against the princes of the northeast. . . . The natives were slaughtered en masse with gun or machine-gun shots. . . . The cruelties inflicted on these people for three months are indescribable. All the crops were burnt . . . the people killed . . . scaffolds were built to hang people upside down, their hands and feet were cut . . . women and especially young girls were mistreated in atrocious ways; some were disemboweled alive; children were torn from their mother's breast and thrown onto the rocks.

After the German defeat in World War I, Belgium claimed Burundi and Rwanda, merging the two former kingdoms into one province and attaching it to their huge colony, the infamous Belgian Congo. The Belgians altered the German approach to ethnicity, corrupting and turning some Tutsi into their servant rulers and evicting the Hutu from all positions of authority, indeed sending many to toil in the mines of

Congo. To establish their rule, the Belgians launched operations they called "police campaigns." Any attempt at protest, even by just a few individuals, could result in punishment for the entire village. Botte describes a police campaign that occurred on November 6, 1919, in retaliation for a Burundian woman's having defended herself from rape:

> The woman wounded the policeman by beating his forehead with her copper bracelets. When her husband heard her cries and came to her rescue, the policeman ran to his station and lied that people wanted to prevent him from cutting the wood. The head of the platoon retaliated with a "police campaign" and took soldiers and policemen and ordered them to burn down the entire hill. A hundred and twenty-three houses were burnt along with ninety-three corn-lofts.

For all the killing they did, the Germans left Burundi's institutions much as they had found them. It was the Belgian colonists, together with Christian missionaries, who deliberately destroyed Burundi's religious, political, and judicial institutions, including that of Bashingantahe.

European missionaries had come to Burundi before the troops, but it was only with the brute force of occupation that they began to convert many Burundians. The Belgian colonial administration banned the practice of the Burundian religion. All of the seasonal and national celebrations, including the blessing of seeds and the festival of harvest, were outlawed. Burundian traditional drumming (which UNESCO later included, for safeguarding, on its Intangible Cultural Heritage of Humanity list) was banned throughout the country for thirty-two years. Any practice of a festive or religious nature was also outlawed. The missionaries imposed a new and foreign term for God and proscribed the Burundian name Imana. Finally, the missionaries, like an occupying army, planted a white flag in the central province of Burundi with an inscription in blue: "Jesus Reigns." In the aftermath of what a Western scholar observed to be collective culture shock, Burundians converted to Christianity en masse. Proud of this mass conversion, something never seen before anywhere else in Africa, one of the missionaries boasted that divine power had hit Burundians like a "tornado of the holy spirit."

After thirty-two years of Christianization, however, another missionary bishop named Julien Gorju wrote with clear regret for what was by then all but destroyed:

The names of God in Burundi are in themselves alone a whole theodicy. . . . They swore by Imana, they filially confided to his Providence, they prayed to him, they thanked him. And these are daily practices, touching in their simplicity: the water of Imana . . . the place of importance given to Imana in the most solemn circumstances of life—the celebration of the newly born, the first fruits of the season, etc. Really if the missionaries encountered beauty anywhere it was here, in this monogamous society, with strict and severe family morals that Islam could not penetrate, a people who, while Europe was unaware of their existence, lived God.

The bishop also wrote: "In the last analysis, religion is to live God, and the grossest consequence of destroying the tradition, was that we sacrificed the Burundian names that are so suggestive: the adages, the wishes filled with the name Imana, that made the life of a Burundian a perpetual communion with the one true God."

Although Bashingantahe was not per se a religious institution, the celebration of a newly anointed Mushingantahe had been a solemn religious occasion. The practice was separate from the king's national administration. Its power was moral, not physical.

When a candidate was being sworn in, the Bashingan-tahe reminded him, "When insulted, you will not respond with an insult: you are no longer a child." The Bashingantahe used a lot of figurative speech, for instance the declaration "You have now swallowed the stone of Bashingantahe." This meant that from now on the Mushingantahe must stand up for peace and justice, and hold that stance as firmly as if he were a rock.

One early European explorer estimated that there was one Mushingantahe for every two hundred Burundian men. He called the institution "profoundly democratic." Reading the recorded oral histories—both in Kirundi and French—I sometimes imagine how it must have been to live in my village when these just and wise people were roaming the paths and the hills, pausing in their own work to sit by invitation inside the village's grass huts, settling family feuds and declaring their formulaic opening remark: "May peace be with us," which was answered with "May peace spread everywhere." Many villages contained a "mound," a hillock or just an open space where a small group of Bashingantahe would address the villagers, preaching their doctrine of peace and sometimes demonstrating it publicly by conducting a sort of trial to solve a local dispute. Imagining this instrument of peace constantly at work all over the country and at all levels of the society, I find myself thinking that civil war would have been nearly impossible in Burundi when the Bashingantahe still lived. One European wrote: "It is incredible how in a society without police, the Bashingantahe managed to maintain social order by their moral authority." In the old myths, the great Mushingantahe Sacega is routinely quoted as saying, "Where there are Bashingantahe, there can be no tragedy."

But they were destroyed. The Belgians decreed that the Bashingantahe no longer could play the role of judges. In the Belgians' new social order, the baton of justice was replaced with the long whip known as the *chicotte*. That is, they continued the tradition of rule by violence that the Germans had established. The German vice governor of Burundi, General Lothar von Trotha, had described his methods of "pacifying" German colonies in Africa in stark terms that now seem ironically prophetic:

The exercise of violence with crass terrorism and even with gruesomeness was and is my policy. I destroy African tribes with streams of blood and streams of money. Only following this cleansing can something new emerge, which will remain.

CHAPTER 4

The War at School

"Peacemakers, like armies, have their own
troops in reserve."

Asvelt and I went to school for a few years in
Mugara, the nearest town to my home village
of Kigutu. In Mugara, there was a woman who had
made herself a fixture at a Pentecostal church, where
she liked to play the role of the prophet Samuel, as if
she were a prophet herself. She would pray that God
destroy "the Philistines." She would do this in the gar-
bled language known as "speaking in tongues." Among
the congregation, many of the Hutus but none of the
Tutsis knew that by "Philistines" she meant Tutsis.
The woman came to be known as Muphilistina—the
lady of the Philistine prayer. Tensions between Hutus
and Tutsis were rising again and would soon erupt
into war. When a high school teacher named Eusebie,
herself a Tutsi, deciphered Muphilistina's coded lan-

guage, she stopped going to that church and prayed at home. When the civil war began, Muphilistina's prayer was answered in Mugara. Only about a dozen Tutsi families lived there, and Hutu militiamen, who called themselves Soldiers of Christ, killed almost all of them in the course of a single night. Those who survived never returned.

About a year later, in Rwanda, to the north, Catholic priests at all levels, including bishops, lent their support to the genocide of 1994. Some even incited massacres—the priest for instance who invited the Tutsis in his parish to take shelter in his church, which was made of stones, and then told the génocidaires, who were waiting with a bulldozer: "Knock it down. We will build another."

Burundi's ethnic civil war had begun six months before Rwanda's genocide, but in Burundi the story was different—at least among most Catholics. Burundi's highest-ranking Catholic, Archbishop Joachim Ruhuna, devoted himself to a search for peace, and many of the country's priests followed his example. Ruhuna did not build his campaign on Christian doctrine. Instead, he reached back into the country's past, to the memory of the Institution of Wisdom, the Bashingantahe—which was different, of course, from Christianity, but for him and others was consistent

with the example of Christ. He saw the Bashingantahe as the essence of Burundi's old and now shattered culture, its *umuco* (pronounced oo-*moo*-cho),
which means "the light." For a Catholic priest, Christ
is "the light of the world," and for Ruhuna, the Bashingantahe had been the smaller lights of the country
who were working in the spirit of that greater light,
and he hoped that something like the institution could
be revived.

He formed a group of leading citizens and asked
them to make a commitment to work together to re-
dress the ethnic divisions, unite the country, and end
the war, just as the Bashingantahe would have done in
the old times. He went out as the committee's emis-
sary, speaking to ordinary citizens, to government officials, and to the officers and troops of both warring
forces—of the Hutu militias and the Tutsi army. He
even went into the forests and countryside to speak to
the rebels in their camps. His own family had been
slaughtered by an angry Hutu mob at the onset of the
war, and some of the killers had actually fled to his
church, along with more than a thousand other terrified civilians. He had protected the killers from the
government army, saying to the Tutsi soldiers, "Those
who have committed crimes will face justice in the
courts, but we must wait for order to return. You can-

not take anyone unless you kill me first." Three years after the start of the war and his campaign, he was shot to death by a group of Hutu militiamen.

But peacemakers, like armies, have their own troops in reserve. In the mountains to the south of Gitega, there was a Dominican priest named Bukuru Zacharie, a friend and protégé of Ruhuna and the principal of what was generally considered the best secondary school in Burundi, the Séminaire de Buta. In Burundi, political entrepreneurs of violence had for decades created false histories to serve their purposes. In response, laws had been passed to ban the politics of identity. They had not ended hostilities but had only driven them underground, where false histories grew increasingly grotesque. These one-sided accounts had surfaced during the electoral campaign of 1993, which had focused on the divisions between Hutus and Tutsis.

At Buta during that time, Zacharie had noticed with alarm that his students had begun to group themselves by ethnicity—in the classrooms, the dining hall, even in the church. And after members of the Tutsi army assassinated the country's elected president, violence erupted throughout Burundi. There was a real threat that Buta, like many other schools, would dissolve or even descend into violence itself.

The students all said they wanted to go home, the Hutus saying they feared the Tutsi soldiers who had come to protect the school, and the Tutsi students saying they were afraid they would be attacked by their Hutu classmates and the school's Hutu neighbors. At different times early on, the Hutu and the Tutsi students gathered in front of the school with their suitcases.

Zacharie tried to calm their fears, promising the boys he would protect all of them, no matter what might happen. He demanded of them, however, that there be sincere collaboration among them and obedience to Buta's code of conduct. Then, leaving the school in the hands of his trusted subordinates, he made a three-day tour of Bururi and Gitega provinces to witness and evaluate for himself the troubles outside the school. What he saw and heard was not encouraging: houses burning, people fleeing on the roads, stories of massacres both of Hutus and Tutsis. He seems to have returned with a clear idea of what he was going to try to accomplish at the school.

Buta was already an academically rigorous school. It kept its students busy with classes in seventeen different subjects, and also with sports and gardening and volunteer work in the community and studies of the old cultural ways. Now Zacharie set out to make

them busier. The news being generally awful and terrifying to many students, he confiscated all the radios.
He allowed the students to watch the news on TV, but
only as a body surrounded by school officials, and he
would discuss the news with them, ignoring the recent but by now universally abandoned laws of the
previous government, which had forbidden open discussion of ethnicity. He tried to explain the deep ori-
gins of the war, how playing politics with ethnicity
had brought the country to this dreadful place. He
told them they should not avoid the subject of ethnic
identity, but rather look beyond it toward the culture,
the light, that ought to unite all Burundians.

In the first four months of his campaign, he super-
vised open debates in which students were allowed to
voice their fears and to describe their ethnic preju-
dices, though without insulting individuals. To his
surprise, both Hutus and Tutsis referred to the year
1972 as a justification for their fears. The events of
that year had been baptized *ikiza*, literally "the
plague" or "the great calamity." Ironically, all public
discussion about it had been banned, so what these
boys knew about 1972 they had learned from their
relatives or friends in privacy—in whispers and in
gossip. Inevitably, what they thought they had learned
was distorted, biased, and incomplete. And yet in the

open debates, the students declaimed these notions with strong conviction, indeed with what Zacharie would describe as "terrible passion," each side describing atrocities that the other side had committed before the boys were even born. For Zacharie, this revealed a deep subconscious injury that had weighed for decades on the nation.

I grew up hearing about *ikiza* from the Tutsi point of view. Years later, during trips I took back to Burundi from college, I interviewed more than two dozen elderly people who had lived through those dreadful events. I also interviewed a man who had been a government minister during that time. And I read every book I could find that even touched on *ikiza* and the events that led up to it. Some of the books I read were in English. The best were written in French by native Burundian authors and scholars, both Hutu and Tutsi. The story is complex, so complex that several books are dedicated entirely to it, including *Burundi 1972: Massacre des Tutsi dans le Sud* by Novat Nintunze and *Burundi 1972: Au bord des génocides* by the famous French historian Jean-Pierre Chrétien. I hope that I managed to follow Father Zacharie's example by gleaning from these sources an impartial understanding of that violent period.

Here is my attempt at a summary. After Burundi gained independence, in 1962, political actors waged various struggles for power. These contests only became ethnic in 1965, when a group of Hutu extremists organized a massacre of Tutsis in the north. The nation's army was predominantly Hutu at the time, but a Tutsi captain named Michel Micombero led the effort to quash the violence, and within a year he had declared himself president and begun purging Hutus from the government, gendarmerie, and army. During the next several years, resentment and anger grew among Hutus, as did fear among Tutsis, who knew the story of how Hutus in neighboring Rwanda had violently overthrown the Tutsis back in 1959. The turmoil in Burundi turned very violent in 1972. An organized rebellion of Hutus went on the attack, killing Tutsis in the south, and Micombero, with his now largely Tutsi army, launched a slaughter of Hutus, including many intellectuals. Some authors call this a "selective genocide." Others, including several Hutu academics, disagree. Regardless, it appears that as many as three hundred thousand Burundians were killed during *ikiza*.

To me, the real issue in this tragedy is the malevolent human thirst for revenge, the very thing that the Bashingantahe would have prevented if only their institution had not been destroyed. As W. H. Auden writes:

> I and the public know what all schoolchildren
>   learn,
> Those to whom evil is done, do evil in return.

But Zacharie wanted to cultivate a different spirit in his students, by turning to the light, *umuco*. He tried in schoolwide meetings and seminars to correct the boys' misconceptions, offering evenhanded accounts of the *ikiza,* which had in fact been a complex as well as a dreadful period, involving not just ethnic but also geographical resentments, competing political interests, and internal political fights on both sides. He devised other ways to cultivate a spirit of unity in the student body with schoolwide readings and seminars on "the light." He also created cultural clubs made up of Hutus and Tutsis and recruited elders from outside the school to teach them the ancient traditions of Burundian drumming and dancing and drama.

Zacharie reasoned that the school's security depended on peace in the neighborhood. He participated in meetings in the villages, intervening whenever the tensions were rising, and he held meetings inside the school where people from the local community and the government and Tutsi soldiers could all discuss their differences.

A report about Zacharie's efforts was broadcast on national TV and radio news. The prime minister visited the school and presented the priest and his students with what in my country was then and always had been a very meaningful gift—nothing less than a beautiful *inyambo* heifer. News of Zacharie's work at the school reached the whole country, including leaders of the most powerful antigovernment Hutu militia, the National Committee for the Defense of Democracy (CNDD). A regiment of CNDD soldiers was dispatched with the main objective of putting an end to Zacharie's experiment. It is said that they traveled, fighting all the way, through the mountains that divide Burundi from Tanzania. By late April of that year, 1997, they had set up camp on the two hills that loom over the school in Buta. Following tradition, students had erected a cross for Easter at the top of the largest of these hills, named Kagomogomo. The militia set up a large cannon right next to the cross. Two days after Easter Sunday, on the early morning of April 30, the Hutu regiment, as Lord Byron writes of the Assyrians, came down like a wolf on the fold.

. . .

On the morning of the previous day, April 29, after the school had gathered as usual to sing the national anthem, the boom of heavy weapons resounded from the hills. Zacharie saw all the students turn spontaneously, with frightened eyes, not toward the sound but toward him. Soon afterward he got in his car and drove to Bururi Centre to ask for military reinforcements to protect the school. There were only eleven soldiers guarding Buta, not nearly enough to resist a heavily armed force of militia. On his way, Zacharie met the governor of Bururi, who said to him, "Monsieur l'Abbé, I was coming to see you. The situation is very grave. The militia is approaching. We must organize ourselves to protect the population." The road was jammed with refugees, mostly women and children, heading away from Buta toward Bururi Centre, and the refugees frightened the governor, who believed that spies for the militia were certainly among them. He told Zacharie that military radios were to be distributed to civilians to communicate with the government soldiers, that local security committees had been formed to work with the Tutsi army, and that these committees had been tasked to organize nocturnal vigils and to stop and frisk any suspicious people they found among the refugees. The governor said he was going to organize this himself in Kiremba, a town near Buta. He also promised to send military reinforcements to the school. Zacharie drove back to Buta feeling reassured.

But by five o'clock that evening no radios had been distributed and no additional soldiers had arrived to guard the school. Zacharie drove toward Bururi again. On his way, he met three military trucks full of heavily armed soldiers, members of the elite special forces of the government army. Were they coming to protect his students? Zacharie asked. Yes, their leader said. And so the priest turned around and followed the trucks. Then, when they were only a quarter of a mile from the school, the trucks stopped. They turned around. Their commander told Zacharie that he had just been ordered by radio to go to Bururi Centre, but he would consult the commandant there and then return to Buta. Zacharie pleaded with him. Would he bring the soldiers to the school first, just so that the students could see them? The commander said he couldn't do that.

Frustrated and worried, Zacharie once again turned around and followed the trucks to Bururi Centre, where after a great deal of pleading he received vague assurances from the governor that he would contact the commandant of the army forces in the region, who would surely send soldiers to the school. Zacharie should wait in the Centre for news. It had not arrived by 8:30 that night. So Zacharie drove back to the school in the dark, passing many army trucks on his way, all heading in the other direction, toward the Centre and away from Buta. He told himself that these must be the reinforcements for the school, and that they would soon be heading to Buta. In his various conversations that day, he had met one officer who had been fighting this CNDD regiment for a week. The officer said that the army had driven the whole force away from Buta, back into the mountains. The officer didn't know it, but this was only half true. Half of the force, two thousand soldiers, had separated from the others and been sent to destroy Buta's example of interethnic harmony.

Zacharie didn't know this either. He clutched the officer's mistaken assurance because there was no other hope within reach. When he got to his office, two student representatives were waiting for him. The spokesman said, "The students sent us to tell you that they are very scared. This evening they couldn't study. They are waiting for you to come and reassure them." Zacharie told them about the events of the day, that an officer fresh from combat with the militia had said that the militia regiment had been driven away. He told them that he had been promised reinforcements, which would come that night. He added that the well-armed soldiers already on campus would be placed at the entrance to the two dormitories, ensuring the students' safety.

"But if the militia installs their weapons on top of Kagomogomo," one of the representatives said, "we will all perish in the dorm!"

Zacharie called for a meeting of the entire school in the building called the Great Hall. There he repeated everything he had said to the representatives, but he could see from the faces in the auditorium that the students were afraid. He invited them to express their fears. One said he had heard a story about someone finding leaflets on a path near the campus, leaflets addressed to the students, that read, "Tomorrow you will share breakfast with the militia." Another student asked, "Monsieur l'Abbé, what should we do if the militia comes into our dorm? Tell us, please."

Zacharie replied, "If the militia attacks, I will be there. I will tell you what to do."

He didn't know what else he could say. It was late, past nine o'clock. He told the students they could sleep until six-twenty the next morning, an extra hour's rest. Zacharie concluded the meeting with a prayer—praying, he later said, with more emotion than he ever had done, blessing his students and the night.

My brother Peter was a student at Buta, in ninth grade. He had come home to Kigutu for one night, after hearing that our family had been attacked. And he had left with Asvelt and me on the following day—another day when our mother spirited us out of the village in filthy clothes, behaving as if we were just going to fetch palm oil, once again instructing us to put on white clothes once we had reached the top of the first mountain. We had parted ways from Peter some hours later, and he had headed back to Buta. Many years afterward, he told me the story of what followed. While I listened, it seemed as if for him it all could have happened yesterday.

When he got back to Buta, Peter realized that the seniors, those in the twelfth and thirteenth grades—really the bosses of the younger students—had been collectively transformed. "The seniors had just finished a spiritual retreat. Some of those guys, before they went to the retreat, were really mischievous. They boycotted the Mass and talked while in church. But after returning from the retreat, it was as if some miracle had happened. They started going into meditation and praying. They would start giving you spiritual advice, and you wondered, *Is this the same person I knew before?*"

It was on the day after Peter returned to the school that the students began to hear gunfire and the booming of what sounded like cannons. At first the noise sounded distant, like faint thunder far away in the mountains. Every day those sounds of war came nearer. After a week of this, by Tuesday, the twenty-ninth of April, anxiety was palpable everywhere on campus. "Myself, I remember I had no energy at all, not a bit," he remembered. "I was supposed to draw a map and get my geography notebook ready for evaluation, but I couldn't even draw a line. I didn't really have any fear of death, I just didn't have any energy."

There were two dormitories at Buta, both a floor above ground level. They were situated in the same building but each had its own staircase. One dorm was for the seniors and the other for all the younger students, the dorm where Peter slept. He remembered: "So we went to bed afraid, and then at five in the morning, exactly around the time when we would usually go to shower, the shooting began. It was really loud and heavy. We hid under our beds. The shooting went on, and we kept comforting ourselves that it must be the special forces that Zacharie had talked about in the meeting. We couldn't look out through the windows because bullets were hitting them, and also hitting the roof, making lots of noise. So we remained under our beds. Then we heard a lot of people screaming and crying out in agony, and we saw lots of water flowing across the floor. Bullets must have hit the big water tank. That's when we realized the guns we were hearing must belong to the militia. And then we started arguing among ourselves, even as we lay under our beds, some saying, 'It is the militia,' and others saying, 'It is the military.' And then, looking out from under our beds, we saw a little man with a gun coming across the floor. He was wearing a military uniform but a shabby hat, which meant he was a militiaman. He did nothing to us. He just looked around and under the beds and then went back to the door, the door to the stairs, the only exit. He stood there, like a guard, blocking our way out.

"Talking frantically to each other, we realized that those we heard screaming in pain must be students in the senior dorm. We understood that if we wanted to live we had to get out. Our dorm was on the floor above our classroom; our windows were about twenty feet above the ground. But there were a lot of Boy Scouts among us, and they started tying ropes and climbing out the windows. There weren't enough ropes for everyone. I climbed up on a bunk bed and smashed a window with my palm. Then I jumped out and landed on my bare feet on the ground, which was littered with the glass I had broken. It cut deep into my toe, but I didn't even feel it at the time. I ran into the vegetable garden behind the dorm. There was shooting everywhere, and the bullets were like bees. So I lay down on a patch of cabbages in a garden of sorghum. Students were running past me in all directions. Several other students my age were lying near me. One was named Donatien. He had an older brother named Jimmy, and Jimmy was a senior. Donatien recited the Ave Maria over and over, interrupting the prayer to say, 'Oh mercy, they must have killed Jimmy.' "

Like the younger students, the seniors had spent an anxious week since their retreat. Those who survived the attack later remembered their lost friends and things they had said to each other in the dorm the night before. Everything they said was colored by the spiritual retreat that had ended only a week ago.

It was a yearly retreat led by professionals in meditation, and it consisted of five days when the seniors had to maintain complete silence, meditating and praying. The event had a profound effect on most of the older students. I know this because some years later I was one of them. We would return from the retreat making all sorts of resolutions—many of them impossible to fulfill. In the beginning, we would act and behave as if our hearts had been purified— showing great affection and humility to others, vowing to help the needy in service of God, praying several times a day. After a few months, a lot of our piety would have worn off. But back on the night before the attack, the retreat was a very recent memory for the seniors—only a week old—and its influence on them was strong.

Jimmy Prudence said to some of the others in the senior dorm, "Why are you so afraid of death? We must pass by death to arrive at celestial life."

Thierry Arakaza hoped to become a Jesuit. Sitting on his bed, he told his friends, "Even if the militia attacks, we are spiritually prepared. Death is a bridge that brings us to God."

Sébastien said to his friends, "It is truly wonderful to pray because you feel transported to another world more beautiful than ours." But he also confided, "I am so scared, I am going to go to the chapel and recite a rosary."

Diomède Ningaza had spent the afternoon listening to refugees from his hometown who were gathered in a temporary camp at Buta. He could not eat afterward.

Ntakiyica Alphonse spent the night before the attack singing softly to himself. Most of his family had already been killed, and it is said that he felt his turn was coming.

Nimubona Prosper had seen workmen clearing some ground earlier that day, and he had panicked, and his friend Nathan had said to him, jokingly: "It's here that you will be buried tomorrow."

Nzisabira Lénine, always at top of his class, opened his Bible and advised the students around him to do likewise: "Friends, we need to prepare to cross this bridge toward heaven. The enemy is at the door." His classmates referred to him as a nerd. Yet on the eve of the attack, he advised them not to bother about studying but to spend their time in prayer.

As he turned in, Remy said to his friends, "See you tomorrow, God willing."

Like the junior students, the seniors were aroused by gunfire around dawn, bullets coming up the stairs and striking the walls just outside their doorway. There were perhaps a hundred beds in the long dorm room. Survivors remembered that students whose beds were near the door ran to the far end of the room and crawled under the beds there, joining the others. They remembered hearing a woman's voice say, "Where are they?" and a man's voice answering, "They are there, Chief."

The militia began shooting into the room. Several of the students under beds were hit and died at once. Some others were wounded. The shooting stopped. A man's voice ordered the students to come out with their hands up. When the students didn't obey, one of the men said, "Take all the time you need to shoot them." Another said, "No, bring the machetes. Let's cut them into pieces."

The students, the ones still alive and the wounded ones able to move, crawled out into the open then. And militiamen herded them into the empty space near the doorway and demanded, "Give us your money." Some students went back to their beds and opened their suitcases and brought back what cash they had. One student told the militiamen that most of them had given their money to one of the priests for safekeeping. At which point, a student named Willermin said to the others, "Let's not say who the priest is. They'll kill him, and they will kill us anyway." He added, as if quoting from a formal text, "Let us die with dignity."

The woman, evidently the militia chief, ordered the students to separate themselves. "Ours here," she said. "Others there." The students didn't move. One of the men clarified the chief's command, pointing to one side, then the other: "Hutus here, Tutsis there."

The students didn't move. Instead, they all, without exception, joined hands. A survivor remembered, "It was a reflex. We held each other tight."

One of the militia sneered at the students. "They deceived you boys."

The chief slapped one of the students in the face, barking, "Hutus here! Tutsis there!" The survivors remembered her voice. She spoke with the Rwandan accent. Still, the students did not move. She grabbed a submachine gun from one of her men and sprayed a bunch of students with bullets. Some fell instantly. Another militiaman came forward, unpinned a grenade, and rolled it toward the feet of the students still standing. The grenade exploded. There were cries, bodies on the concrete floor, blood and human tissue spattered everywhere. Several had died before the grenade was used, and now at least another fifteen had joined them.

Wounded survivors remembered one student quoting Jesus on the cross as he himself died: "Forgive them, Father, for they know not what they do." Other students, dying on the concrete floor, joined voices, singing psalms. Still others lay there reciting the rosary. One wounded survivor remembered that, in the midst of the singing and prayers, he heard a militia-man say, "Why are we killing these children?" Other militiamen yelled at him, took him out of the room, and shot him there, at the head of the stairs. The students who were able ran back to the far end of the room. The Rwandan woman ordered the troops to fire, saying, "Do it fast! Do it fast!"

The two thousand soldiers of the half regiment were apparently undisciplined. They spent four hours on the campus and could easily have murdered all the students, but they spent much of their time and effort ransacking the campus, shooting at everything and nothing, and collecting beer. There was a store next to the school that sold beer. The militia carried away the entire contents of the store, thousands of bottles. Finally, they returned to the hilltops. From the campus below, survivors saw militiamen danc-ing, and students the militia had kidnapped later reported that the soldiers spent the next few hours celebrating.

Some of the survivors were seniors the militia had left on the floor under their beds, assuming they were dead. When the soldiers first left the dorm, those stu-dents crawled out and tried to help the others, using their training in first aid, binding wounds to stop the bleeding, administering mouth-to-mouth resuscitation. In many cases, these were Hutus trying to save Tutsis and Tutsis trying to save Hutus in interethnic acts of bravery. The Bashingantahe would have been proud of them. Several times militiamen returned to the dorm, checking to see if any of the wounded students were still breathing, some of them trying to lure out students who were feigning death by saying in soft voices, "Oh, does anyone need help?" This happened several times, with wounded students crawling out to try to help the dying, then crawling back under the beds when they heard the militiamen returning. Most made it back under the beds in time, but some were caught and shot to death. Half an hour after the militia troops left the school at last, the government army arrived. Doctors and medics and ambulances soon followed.

Peter remembered: "There comes a time when fear goes away, and the mind keeps racing. You keep thinking about different things. I remembered people saying that bullets shot into a banana plant don't go through it because when the bullets reach the water inside the stem, they get wet and are extinguished. Just as this memory entered my mind, I got up from the sorghum garden and ran into the banana grove beside it, where I could actually hide. I felt something hit me but it was pieces of the cabbages I had been lying on, hit by a shell from the cannon up on the hill above the school. If I had waited only a few seconds, the shell would have killed me. I hid in the banana grove but I was too scared to stay. Bullets were hitting the fronds all around me. I started to run. I ran past a boy named Oscar. Do you remember the names on the graves? There was a boy named Oscar. He had been hiding with me, but they had shot him in the stomach. He was desperate, and he was walking toward the militia, shouting. I think he wanted the militia to hear him and finish him off. Several other students and I ran the other way, toward the eucalyptus forest, and I never saw Oscar again. When I got to the top of the road, I saw houses burning, and there were many soldiers, all militia. I hid briefly beside the road and waited for them to go by, and then I sprinted across the road into the banana plantation and went on running towards Grandma in Mahonda. I ran and ran and ran."

If one were walking fast, without a wound in one's foot, that trip home would take about four hours. The way Peter told the story, it took all the time in the world and no time at all. When he arrived, he found our sister Daphrose and our uncle Didace chatting with our grandmother.

"When Grandma saw me, she asked where I had come from, and I said Buta, and she said, 'I had forgotten that you go to school there.' I told them the militia had attacked Buta and that I had just narrowly escaped. I don't remember much, really. I do remember where Grandma and Didace and Daphrose were standing and their gestures—Grandma saying she'd forgotten that I went to school at Buta and Daphrose staring at me with frightened eyes, but I don't remember anything else after that. All I know is I had lost my mind. So I ran back towards Bururi. When I arrived in the town center, I met, I think, some relatives of our cousin Grace, and I got into a military vehicle and went down to Rumonge and went straight to the military camp and stayed for a few days with Grace's father, who commanded a platoon. And then I went down to Bujumbura and stayed with Uncle Nestor, and then I stayed with Boniface maybe? I don't really remember much. From what I recall, nothing followed after the attack, nothing happened. Days passed. And school resumed, and I went back. That's all I remember."

In a book he later published, *The Forty Young*

Martyrs of Buta, Zacharie recounts how he hid in his office during the assault and emerged after the militia had left, when another priest came looking for him. Zacharie asked him, "What about my boys?" And the priest replied, weeping, "They are dead." Zacharie later wrote that he felt he had been stabbed in his heart.

Shortly afterward, Zacharie and his superior, Bishop Bernard Bududira, applied to the Vatican for support in creating a monument to the murdered students, and their plea was quickly answered. The result was a second church on the campus of Buta, a rather lovely church, its open courtyard filled with forty purple coffins. I remember attending mandatory Sunday services there when I was a student.

During the war Zacharie did some brave and very risky things. Several years after the massacre he assembled the funds to build a monastery next to the memorial church, where he intended to live the rest of his life in silence. I think of this as his act of penance, to live beside his martyred students, who were so much braver than he, so much braver in truth than the vast majority of us. To the church, they are Christian martyrs. Most important to me, they are also latter-day Bashingantahe.

CHAPTER 5

The Color of a Sound

"Kill them slowly one after another."

"*Kamwe kamwe ku ruyeri ku rwembe.*" The song's melody sounded so beautiful on that Tuesday in April 1997, one of the days my mother apologized to Asvelt and me for having brought us into the world. I remember her saying to us: "Why did I give birth to you, my dear children? Forgive me. I didn't know Burundi was going to turn into this."

We were at our house trying to decide whether to go to the forest as we usually did at night to hide from the rebels. After four years of this, we did not mind the rain in the forest anymore. But that evening, Asvelt, maman, and I didn't feel like leaving our house, because a storm was coming. The sky had turned dark, lightning came from all directions, and we told ourselves that the rumbles we heard were thunder, not guns. It looked as if it was going to rain hard. Almost always at this hour, we were already in the forest.

"What if we wait for the rain to pass?" Asvelt suggested.

"Who knows that it won't rain through the night as usual?" my mother asked.

We all stayed mute and waited. And then we heard a group of people singing that song I thought was so beautiful. I didn't understand the lyrics. It was a type of song I knew, *urukato,* usually sung during communal work—while clearing a road or working on a construction site. I later learned that the work it was supposed to accompany that evening was killing people. Its words figuratively mean, "Kill them slowly one after another." I didn't know this, of course, and I didn't know that it was a group of rebels who were singing the words. I started humming the tune.

As the voices drew nearer, maman asked me, "What are you singing?"

I said, "I don't know. It sounded so good that I found myself repeating it."

She looked worried. "I doubt this song. Who do you think these people are? We better go out. What is the meaning of that song?"

We became afraid. But it was too late for us to run

away. We heard people in front of the house talking to each other, saying, "This time we will get them." We rushed out our back door. There were several trees of God nearby, and we lay on the ground beneath them. From there, we could hear everything, and lifting our heads, we could see, in the dim light, that one of the rebels had gone inside our house, which had six rooms. The man must have been a commander, because when he came back outside, he said in a loud voice, "I want six people and each one for his room!"

"I don't want to be slaughtered," Asvelt whispered. "I am going to run, and they will shoot."

I told him to calm down and wait. They hadn't seen us, and it was getting dark.

Looking in the direction of the main path of the village, I saw militiamen marching in what looked like endless lines. Looking back toward our house, I saw the soldiers going inside and in a little while coming out carrying our clothes and food. Then we heard the commander shout, "Get out of the house and open fire!"

They threw grenades into the house and then fired their rifles at it, and the brick walls crumbled.

Then we heard another volley of gunshots in the distance. And soon after that, chaos: all the rebels started shooting at government soldiers who had arrived and were shooting too. It was dark by now, and under cover of this cacophony of guns, we scurried farther from our house and crowded into a thicket. They fought all night long, the government soldiers advancing, the rebels retreating. One single night seemed a century, but it passed, and we passed through it.

By morning the government soldiers had reached our village. I hoped for safety, but it had not arrived yet. To the south of the village, the sounds of battle continued. At the base of the mountains, government planes were dropping bombs. We didn't know where to flee. So we stayed in the village. We walked around the ruins of our house, looking for a place to hide. Our village lay along a main route for the rebels. This meant that many battles were staged near Kigutu and in the town of Mugara, where we went to school. In my memory, the aftermath of these fights was always dreadful—the town smelling of death, children crying over corpses, trying to wake their dead mothers. Even animals became victims. I remember seeing dead antelopes and goats, and cows with their legs amputated, bleeding and crying out. Everything was in pain and mourning. I was eight, and it felt to me as if a crime had been committed against creation itself.

At twilight the government soldiers, our protection, began to retreat under fire. As they passed by the ruin of our house, several of them said we should leave the village at once. Among the soldiers was a student who had recently graduated from high school. (During the war, you had to serve in the army before going to college.) This boy had not eaten breakfast and had been fighting all day long. I think a mixture of fear and hunger made him collapse by the side of the main village road. He lay there so traumatized and exhausted that he couldn't retreat with the other soldiers. While his comrades were discussing how to carry him, their commander ran up and ordered them to shoot the student, saying that he might give away secrets if the militia found him. The soldiers protested, so the commander took the student's gun and left him there unarmed. The militia was advancing, and it was getting dark. I felt terrible for the young man. But what could I do?

As the soldiers hurried away in retreat, maman overheard some of them talking about the student they had left behind. Had they done something wrong? Maman asked them what had happened, they explained, and she turned back, heading for the student, toward the advancing militia.

I heard one of the soldiers ask another, "Why are we running away with guns when she is going back without one?"

Asvelt and I ran after her, begging, "Please, Maman, come back!"

But she said, "Do not follow me. Keep running. I cannot leave that child behind. If he had a mother, she wouldn't let him be slaughtered."

To me just then, this was maddening. The attack we had just escaped had been led by a man named Sironi, a rebel and a neighbor whom maman had hidden in our house and fed when government soldiers were chasing him. She had done that only a few months ago, and yet Sironi had led his fellow militia in an attempt to kill us. I had hoped that would be a lesson for my mother, but it wasn't the kind of lesson she believed in. We kept begging her. We said, "Maman, why do you want us to be killed?" But she refused to come back until she had cared for the student.

On the occasions when we were forced to run away and hide, Maman Clémence would carry a heavy bag full of food, because we never knew when we would be returning home. She was carrying the bag now, and when she reached the student, she fed him something—I don't remember just what. And the food or her attention or both quickly revived him, enough that he was able to get up and walk on with us to a hiding place before the militia arrived.

I was happy the student had been saved, but I wanted my mother to remember Sironi. I wanted her to realize that she shouldn't hide people who might later kill us. I said, "Maman, why do you make us sleep and share food with people who come back to kill us?"

"Are you afraid this kid is going to kill you?" she said. "He is miserable, just as you are."

"I don't mean him, but how about Sironi?"

"The problem then is, you can't tell. I did my duty. Children look the same."

"If you don't know the person, then you don't know! You can't trust everyone you meet on the road!" I said.

"Did the people who took Deo in know him?" she replied. She was referring to an older brother, by then living with a family in America. "Were they his parents?" she asked. "His siblings? His relatives?"

What she was doing was dangerous, I thought, but I kept a chastened silence. She broke it after a while, saying, "Let this difficult life teach you, too."

I didn't try to give her back an answer. I didn't have one.

That night we slept in a small thick woods of pine trees situated a few kilometers from our ruined house. A dirt road bordered the woods. When morning came, I got up and went to pee, and looking through the trees, I saw five uniformed men out in the open on that road. I could hear their voices clearly. They were shouting toward the woods, saying that people should come out, they were safe now. I knew it was a trap. The government soldiers had run away hours ago. Then off to my right I saw someone, a boy, come out from the trees and onto the road. I recognized him. It was Patrick, a schoolmate who was twelve. He ran toward the uniformed men. He didn't know they were rebel soldiers. He must have forgotten that militiamen looked like other human beings. Four of them were sitting by the side of the road. One leaned against a tree, holding a water glass that he had probably stolen from a house nearby.

Patrick ran up to him. I could hear him; he was breathing hard. The soldier with the glass asked, "Why are you running?"

Patrick pointed back toward the village, where smoke was still rising from the burning houses. "Look!" he said.

"Sit down and catch your breath. You're safe now."

I was only about five meters from them, close enough that I could see there was a little liquid left in the soldier's glass. Also close enough to be afraid, to feel I must not make a sound. I held my breath and tightened all my muscles.

The rebel dropped the glass—I'm sure it was on purpose. I heard the glass shatter, and I saw pieces of the broken glass on the ground—I seem to remember that they were glinting in the morning sun.

The rebel looked down at those shards, and he said to Patrick, "Boy, you were asking me to share, weren't you?" According to an old Burundian joke, if you dropped something you were eating or drinking, the person next to you was to blame; that is, you dropped it because the other person was jealous and wanted a share. The rebel smiled at Patrick. "Take and eat," he said.

I think it was then that Patrick realized that this was a militiaman. I could see that he had started trembling.

"Collect those pieces of glass and put them in my hand!" said the commander. Patrick bent down and did as he was told.

"Open your mouth!" the rebel said.

Patrick shook his head. I could see his hands trembling.

The militiaman held his submachine gun in one hand and pressed the barrel against Patrick's forehead, and he said, "You choose. You open, or I shoot." Patrick opened his mouth, and the rebel shoved the pieces of glass inside it. "Close your mouth and chew!" Patrick's mouth was too full to make a chewing motion, so the soldier put down his gun, took my friend's head in his hands, and forced his jaws together. Patrick chewed once more and spit out blood. The soldier picked up his gun and shot Patrick once between the eyes.

During the war, I had seen many other killings, some of them even more horrifying than Patrick's. Eleven years later, I went to the United States to spend a year at a boarding school called Deerfield Academy, in western Massachusetts. By then, I had buried the memory of Patrick's murder. But early in my year at Deerfield, Patrick returned. In the dining hall, students sometimes would drop a glass or plate by mistake, and whenever I heard glass breaking, I did not think of the old Burundian joke, I didn't think someone had wanted to share another's drink, I thought of Patrick's mouth full of glass and would see him trying to chew. My mouth would be full of food, and I could not chew it. It was as if I were still watching Patrick. It was as if the food in my mouth had become the slivers of glass and I felt them slicing my gums. It was as if I were eating his blood. It was as if I were still running away in a war that had not ended.

When my fellow students at Deerfield heard the sound of glass breaking, they knew that someone had dropped a glass and they would laugh at that person's clumsiness. Innocent laughter, in which I couldn't join. When I heard the sound of a glass breaking, I would see a red color. The color of blood in Patrick's mouth. A color no one else could hear.

Umuco

"We can easily forgive a child who is afraid
of the dark; the real tragedy of life is when
men are afraid of the light."

In Burundi, as in Rwanda, the word for culture is *umuco,* literally, "the light." Before I came to America, I went to a retreat center and spent a week in silence. My hope was to find *umuco* for myself and my country. When I got to the States, I studied political science and psychology, hoping they would be the right tools for my quest. In the process, I read Plato's *Republic,* and I was struck by one of the dialogues:

Socrates: Sight may be present in the eyes and the one who has it may try to use it, and colors may be present in things, but unless a third kind of thing is present, which is naturally adapted for this purpose, sight will see nothing, and the colors will remain unseen.

Plato: What kind of thing do you mean?
Socrates: I mean what you call the light.

Later in the dialogue, the discussion goes:

Socrates: When we turn our eyes to things whose colors are no longer in the light of day but in the gloom of night, the eyes are dimmed and seem nearly blind, as if clear vision were no longer in them. Yet whenever one turns them on things illuminated by the sun, they see clearly, and vision appears in those very same eyes.
Plato: Indeed.
Socrates: Well, understand the soul in the same way: When it focuses on something illuminated by truth and what is, it understands, knows and apparently possesses understanding, but when it focuses on what is mixed with obscurity, on what comes to be and passes away, it opines and it is dimmed, changes its opinion this way and that, and it seems bereft of understanding.

I had wanted to describe the light, *umuco,* in my writing. But when a country has descended into great darkness, as Burundi has since its civil war, how do you find the light, how do you bring it back? I had come to feel that the light and writing are a gift of God wrapped in thorns and that to retrieve it is to endure. I found myself incorporating prayer in my attempts.

I had recently returned to the Catholic church and had asked for a sacrament of reconciliation. It took me a while to admit it, but I had renounced God in my heart for the past ten years here in America, the most tumultuous part of my life. A priest in Brooklyn welcomed me back, administered absolution—a formal release from guilt—and then invited me for a Eucharist, adding that I should try to come for Communion at least once a week, every Sunday if I could. Easy, I thought. I had been required to go to Mass every day for five years at Buta Catholic school back home in Burundi. And back then I had been obliged to wake up at five-twenty in the morning, in order to attend. I decided now to start going to Mass every day again, at St. Patrick's in Brooklyn, about a fifteen-minute walk from my apartment. It was a good discipline, spiritually and in other ways. I remember myself at Buta—I felt centered then.

The Catholic Mass is structured so that the first reading comes from the Old Testament, the second from the New Testament, and the priest's reading comes from the Gospels of Matthew, Mark, Luke, or John. After the ser-

mon come the Prayer of the Faithful and general inter-
cessions, to which the congregation responds with
"Lord, hear our prayer."

On my first day of Mass, the first reading was from
the Old Testament book of Samuel. Listening to that first
reading, something about church in general started
bothering me again, something about the prophet Samuel's saying a prayer of intercession, asking God to inter-
vene on behalf of the Israelites against the Philistines. I
couldn't believe I was hearing this story again, on the
very first day of my return. This same biblical story had
been used against my people, in a very twisted way.

A lot of killings happen in Samuel, as they often do
in the stories of the Old Testament. But I didn't know
that this particular reading was going to drag on for two
weeks. *Every single day, for fourteen days straight,* I was
listening to the story of the Philistines and the prophet
Samuel. Why, I asked myself, am I voluntarily torturing
myself with this nightmare? Really, the first time I return
to the church, I'm welcomed with this? Is this a devil's
setup, or what? I felt tempted to abandon church again.
But I told myself, No, I am going to renew my relation-
ship with my God. After all, this was part of the retribu-
tion for my sins. When the priest administers absolution,
he also acts as if he were your disciplinarian and suggests some brief form of self-inflicted punishment—in

my case attending Mass at least once every week—and you are advised to make the occasion a turning point and to do so with firm resolution. I made it through the first week of Mass. I was glad. But the second week? I had to listen to the continuing story, from the second book of Samuel. It's a long story, the story of the Israelites at war with the Philistines.

Every day for those two weeks, when the priest at Saint Patrick's finished his sermon and we came to the responsive parts of the Prayer of the Faithful, I had difficulty bringing myself to join others in saying, "Lord, hear our prayer." My mind was traveling between Saint Patrick's and another church back home, and I felt irritated. I reluctantly joined the others in saying, "Lord, hear our prayer," but I mumbled the words, as if I didn't agree.

CHAPTER 6

Coming to America

"Going back to fix Burundi was my
American dream."

A few weeks before coming to America, I felt a
sudden fear. Until then I had been a quiet and
confident student, and I was eager to further my studies and to be reunited with Asvelt, who had gone to
the United States a year before and was now studying
at Williams College. It seemed strange that I would
suddenly be afraid. I tried to name the cause but
couldn't. It wasn't exactly the fear of venturing into
the unknown, but something like a premonition that
I might get lost in whatever it was. I returned to the
retreat center in Giheta, to the same place where seniors at Buta spent a week in meditation and prayer. I
went back there for another week, but alone this time,
to confront my premonition in silence and with
prayer.

One of my older brothers, Deo, was already a permanent resident of the United States and on his way to becoming a citizen. He had been a medical student in Burundi when the civil war broke out. He had made a long and narrow escape from the war and had ended up in New York City, where a couple had taken him in and where he had managed to enroll at Columbia University. He had returned to Burundi several times while I was still at Buta, and with the help of American friends he had begun to create an organization called Village Health Works and to transform my native village of Kigutu—building not just a hospital but also schools and a hydroelectric plant, and even a Catholic church, which was named after the priest philosopher Saint Thomas Aquinas.

On one of those trips, Deo visited Asvelt and me at Buta. He came with an American man who, Asvelt noticed, carried a notebook and seemed to be constantly writing in it. Asvelt was sure that this man was a CIA agent. He seemed to observe and note the smallest details, as if to him, everything and everyone was an important source of information. Could he be investigating the murder of the students at Buta a decade ago? But what interest would an American have in this?

I noticed that he exchanged greetings with both

hands, in the customary Burundian manner of extreme courtesy, even bowing to peasants with the utmost politeness. I remember shaking hands with him, but I didn't speak. At the time, I didn't know any English. As I later learned, this suspected spy was actually an American author named Tracy Kidder, and he was following Deo to gather details for a book he later published titled *Strength in What Remains*. First for Asvelt and then for me, he became the path to America. (We called him Tracy at home, but I liked the tone of his last name, Kidder.)

We had been eyeing some universities in Europe, because if you had top grades on a national-level exam, you could be awarded a government scholarship to study abroad, and Asvelt and I had done well. I hadn't thought of America, but because of Deo, going to university there had become a dream of Asvelt's.

I didn't know what steps Kidder took, only that they succeeded, in part. He didn't get Asvelt into a university right away. Instead, Asvelt would spend a year boarding at Deerfield Academy on full scholarship. He would be enrolled there in a postgraduate program that prepared students with extra coursework geared toward college. Kidder managed all this with a great deal of help from the associate head of the academy, a woman named Marty Lyman, who had traveled in Africa and was eager to bring international students to the school. Asvelt would board there, but Kidder and his wife lived nearby and would act as Asvelt's host family.

When Asvelt was admitted to Deerfield, I was happy for him, but also sad to see him leave. We had been stapled together throughout the long decade of war, and it seemed as though neither of us could imagine a life without the other. I remember that my graduation ceremony from Buta fell on the same day as Asvelt's departure. I skipped graduation and went with him to the airport. I later learned that it wasn't long after he got to Deerfield that Asvelt began talking about me to the Kidders. And soon, without telling them first, he went to the admissions office and asked if I could apply. The answer was promising, but for him it also felt like a challenge. He was told that because he and I came from the same background, my chances would be greater if he did well during this year at Deerfield.

Afterward, he told the Kidders what he had done. And he studied hard. I suppose he did this for both of us. He had come to America with very little English, but by the end of the school year his grades placed him among the top ten students of the senior class. He had high grades in math and chemistry, where English wasn't as much of a barrier as in other subjects. His year at Deerfield ended well for both of us. He graduated cum laude. Admissions accepted my application and gave me a scholarship. And the Kidders signed papers to serve in loco parentis for me as they had for Asvelt.

I didn't know the meaning of the Latin term in loco parentis when I first heard it, but I deduced that it meant the sort of family that international students are matched with when they leave their home to study abroad. When I later searched for its exact meaning, I learned that the term means "in the place of a parent." So the Kidders had signed the Deerfield forms to stand in the place of Maman Clémence.

Back home in Burundi there was a sad expression that was like a warning to those who leave their family and friends and embark on a long journey to a place far from home. In translation that place is "The faraway land of whom can I talk to, where the cries of a child cannot reach the mother's ears." Looking back, as I think about this expression and the time we spent with the Kidders, I realize now that when the Kidders signed the Deerfield forms, they also signed in their hearts, in the hope that we might never know this Burundian expression while we studied in America.

Kidder was married to an artist, a beautiful lady with red hair, named Frances. Their children were both adults and had long since left home. They lived in a small town in western Massachusetts, and they also had a summer place on the coast of Maine. I spent some time with them there before school started at Deerfield.

The house was built beside a small harbor called Seal Cove. It had a tower with a bedroom where I studied English and slept. I liked to see the tree branches at eye level and the waters of the cove so close below from my bed, in moonlight or during the day. I felt imbued with nature. Oftentimes in the late afternoon Kidder went out fishing for sport, and he'd always invite me to go with him. Sometimes we'd go for a boat ride north of the cove, far out into the ocean. I recall these moments with fondness. When the sea was tranquil, he'd let me steer the boat. I spent about three weeks there, and then they drove me back to their main house in Williamsburg, to get me ready for Deerfield, a twenty-minute drive away.

The house was filled with books. When all was quiet and no one was at home, I felt as if I were in a small library, decorated with paintings—some of which had Frances's signature—and Kidder's literary awards, which included a Pulitzer Prize. Every morning the Kidders woke up reading. They had a fixed routine. Around six, Kidder drove to the store to get the newspapers. Then he made coffee and did his *New York Times* crossword puzzle. They usually had breakfast around seven, and then they read until they parted company for the day, Kidder to his writing office in the basement, and Frances to her painting studio by the Mill River, in the Arts and Industry Building in a town called Florence. There was a tranquility about those days that reminded me of the quiet times at Buta.

I knew almost nothing of the country's history and even less of its culture. Small things puzzled me, trivial things—Americans waved hello and goodbye in exactly the way people back home gestured when they needed help and wanted you to come quickly; for a while I kept getting lost on Deerfield's campus. But I didn't pay much attention to those things. From the time I arrived, I had known one basic fact: America was a country full of resources and opportunities. And I assumed that the people here had created this magnificent country through education and sheer hard work. I also imagined that most American high schools were as richly endowed as Deerfield, with its libraries and laboratories and playing fields. Deerfield astonished me. To grow up here with all these books!

My fellow students had to be walking libraries. I thought that if I really focused my mind and worked harder than ever before, I could fully educate myself and return home equipped to fix and transform my country. I imagined I would make friends here and invite them to Burundi to help me in my quest. I wished I was fluent in English, but the language problem just meant I would have to work harder. I knew young people liked to send texts, so I asked the Kidders to block my phone from receiving them, to protect myself from being distracted. (I remember that after my graduation from Williams five years later, I went to a Verizon store with Frances to have my phone unblocked. The technician looked bewildered. He'd never heard of anyone blocking texts, so he had to search online to figure out how to do it.)

At Williams I was by chance drawn to psychology, which I studied with a professor named Laurie Heatherington. In Burundi, mental health was a subject only for the educated people of the city. I had grown up ignorant of it, but I soon realized that it would be of great importance in the rural parts of the country, too. I had spent the year between graduation and Deerfield working for Deo and his American friends at Village Health Works, which offered only primary medical care. I thought a mental health program should and could be added, so I decided I would study the subject so I could figure out how to build such a program. Laurie was eager to help with this project. (After several years of work, we published our studies in the *Journal of Transcultural Psychiatry*.)

My immigration lawyer had offered to put me on a path to citizenship but I had resisted, saying that I planned to return home. I didn't tell him that going back to fix Burundi was my American dream. Laurie fed me books about psychology, and as I read, I wondered how one would deliver Western treatments for mental illness to rural people in Burundi. First of all, obviously, one would have to understand their thinking. Laurie and I worked out a plan. I executed the first step sophomore year, flying back to Burundi during the college's monthlong winter recess. I stayed at Maman Clémence's house near Village Health Works, which by now had become a tidy group of concrete buildings with tiled floors and open to the air, where about a hundred people came every day for treatment. The staff and I brought small groups of willing patients to the community center, where they sat on chairs while I asked them questions about mental health in general. Most of them spoke about three kinds of illness, all of which seemed to translate well to Western categories—*akabonge* (depression), *guha-*

hamuka (PTSD), and *ibisigo* (psychosis). The following summer I went back and validated the connections between each set of terms: I would give them the Kirundi names of those ailments and ask them to describe the symptoms, and then I would do the opposite, describing the Western version of the symptoms, and ask the group for the Kirundi names that stood for them.

For the final part of the project, Laurie assembled descriptions of what were generally considered the most effective treatments for depression, PTSD, and psychosis. I translated these, and we devised a questionnaire that asked the respondents if they thought those treatments would be effective and whether they would consider undergoing any of them. On my next trip back, I rented a car and provided the questionnaire to contacts I had made in each of Burundi's seventeen provinces. These people agreed to distribute the questionnaire, and I arranged to collect the replies. In all, about a thousand people responded. I also went to Village Health Works and interviewed patients, asking them the same questions and writing down their answers.

Some of what they said surprised me. The treatments I described for PTSD and depression included both talk therapy and exposure therapy. Each of them in different ways involves revisiting the sources of the trouble. I didn't think many of my fellow Burundians would even consider doing that. Kirundi contains not just one but two terms for reminding a person of something unpleasant; both terms are active verbs and signify committing acts that are impolite and even cruel. And indeed, some respondents said they wouldn't consider such treatments—several said that would be "like piercing a scar." But the terms refer to acts committed in normal conversation, not for therapy, and a majority of the respondents understood this distinction. They believed that those sorts of treatments would be both acceptable and effective.

During my first informal study, in assembling terminology, I also asked those groups of mountain people what kind of treatment they would seek for depression and PTSD and pyschosis. Many spoke about *gusenga,* which I vaguely understood as "spiritual healing." I thought the details would be simple. I was much more interested in learning what the schools of medicine and psychology were teaching. This led me back to Bujumbura, the capital city. It looked much the same to me as before the war had ended. It was still divided by ethnicity and between the wealthy and the poor, and compared to Boston or New York it was almost a small town or, really, a low-roofed, single-story city with neighborhoods of unpaved roads and visible scars of war, as at the medical school, where one building still bore cracks in its walls from artillery fire. Walking through its campus, I found myself thinking again about the wealth of resources at American schools.

At the University of Burundi, I visited professors of psychiatry and clinical psychology and a priest who taught anthropology. Both of the clinicians were teaching a Western understanding of psychology, but they and the anthropologist all told me that they had done research on the old spiritual healing of mental illness, and all three said they believed that it was more effective than what they were teaching.

Each of the main three illnesses—Burundi's versions of depression, psychosis, and disorders caused by trauma—had its own therapy, but all the therapies shared certain protocols. These were elaborate. After giving consent, the patient had to go through an intense spiritual experience that involved six stages. These involved purification—the therapist sprinkling a liquefied medicine called *umuhozo* on the patient's head, shoulders, chest, wrists, and ankles. A massage followed, and then a ritualized death and rebirth during which the patient was said to have gone on "a journey." The patient lay naked and silent in a dark room for three days, visited only by a trusted godparent, a *nyenibanga,* who would bring a small portion of bitter greens. On the fourth day, the patient was awakened and dressed in brand-new clothes. A woman patient would also be adorned with ornaments called *ibirezi*—pearls. The patient was then taken to the top of a hill to rest beside a sacred shrub, breathing fresh air and experiencing a transcendent feeling, while the family and spiritual therapist prepared a meal of vegetables. They also picked tall, green, pleasant-smelling herbs grown especially for the ritual and added them for flavor, the way rosemary is added to bean soup.

The entire therapy lasted five days and nights. On the next to last evening, an odd sort of party was held. The patient didn't drink alcohol, but the others did, and were instructed to break rules of decorum, to engage in complaining, deriding others, cursing, and so on. This was intended to allow patients to feel free to speak any thoughts that they would otherwise have repressed, and to cry and yell if they felt like doing so. The second and last purification came on the fifth day and involved a procession to a river—there are many rivers in Burundi—singing, sprinkling of river water on the patient, and ritual bathing. Then the patient would cross the water to the other side of the river, and the whole therapy group would climb to the top of a hill where the patient would plant all three species of the tree of God. At the end of it all, the patient received various gifts, usually a heifer and a white sheep, and was also awarded a gift of responsibility—a communal job to perform, helping others in the village.

The professors had given me various written accounts of this ancient spiritual healing. As I read, I remembered a time when I had just begun working on this book and had felt in need of getting some of that older Burundian therapy myself. And in a sense I did that. Among various options, the old therapy advised that a patient be referred to the Bashingantahe. I called Asvelt, whom I saw as a Muganantahe, a rising member of the Institution of Wisdom.

I complained to him over the phone, saying that I was living a shitty life. This greatly upset him, partly because I had told him that thoughts of suicide visited me often. He texted me in the middle of that night:

I kept thinking about what you said which bothered me. Your life is not "shitty." It's a gift. Maybe the choices and therefore the thoughts you're entertaining are. If you receive a gift and you don't use it for its intended purpose, does the gift lose its intrinsic value? Do you throw it away just because you don't know how to use it or the purpose it serves? I'm not thinking about the grandiose philosophical question about the purpose or meaning of life. It's only an analogy that helps to characterize the problem. For every problem, there is more than one way to look at it. I would just ask you this: are you so sure this is the only way to look at it? Is life itself even the problem? Or maybe the mess it's in, in which case the right question would be: what can I possibly do to get out of that mess? What you said reminded me of reflections I used to immerse myself in. The conclusion I drew was that the problem I was dealing with was twofold: either I was asking the wrong question, in which case the answer was useless, or I was asking the right question but did not genuinely want the answer. The real and satisfactory answer will come from within you. But you have to make sure you are asking a relevant question.

It is one thing to contemplate finding ways to help people recover from the psychological injuries of war. It is another to imagine yourself helping a country mend itself politically. While I was driving around Burundi on the psychology project, I was also trying to learn all I could about my country and the surrounding region. At one point, I traveled into eastern Congo, which seemed to be in a state of perpetual conflict— a dangerous and not very productive trip. I made the mistake of telling Kidder about it, and he made me promise that I wouldn't visit Congo again.

At Williams I was studying political science even more avidly than psychology. I was looking for an example of enlightened political leadership. On my trips back to Burundi, I was mainly trying to learn all I could about that old institution. The American ambassador and his wife arranged for me to meet various former officials in the capital, including one elderly doctor who had gone to school and worked with Prince Louis Rwagasore—the father of Burundi's independence and its first elected prime minister. He was beloved by Hutus and Tutsis alike, and was murdered before he could take office—the paid assassin was a Greek hired, it is widely believed, by the Belgians and their allies among the prince's relatives. Remnants of the Bashingantahe had trained and advised Rwagasore. The elderly doctor talked to me for hours about that training and about how Rwagasore and his team had managed to unite the country, in spite of the Belgians' long-standing attempts to divide it. And he referred me to other former officials who spoke to me about how everything came apart after the assassination. Some of them gave me copies of original documents from that period and also copies of their own unpublished memoirs. The ambassador's wife, Jennifer Watson, contacted other embassies in Burundi to help me in my research, and through Laurie and the librarians at Williams, I was able to get—from Germany, Belgium, and France—copies of what the missionaries had written about Burundi and the Bashingantahe.

But I found the richest material on the ground. During my winter and summer trips, I visited people my friends and acquaintances had said I should interview. Sometimes I would stop to talk to people by the roadsides, especially those who looked old enough to have heard stories from their parents about the old culture—the *umuco,* which they described with a vocabulary that was now rare and fading. Some remembered stories their parents told about the Bashingantahe in action, settling disputes, keeping the peace, preserving order. And when they spoke about them this way, they used the adjective *intwari,* an untranslatable term of praise that seemed to have died along with the Bashingantahe.

Back at Williams, I read many books foreign scholars had written about Burundi. I learned something from every one of them. I felt grateful to the authors, and yet none of these books mentioned Burundi's culture, the *umuco* and the Bashingantahe. They didn't even describe the simple traditions having to do with cows. Historians and anthropologists make a fuss about original sources. "Very original indeed," I remember saying quietly to myself, after arguing with one scholar I would rather not name. I thought that some of the books he relied on ought to be classified as historical fiction. How could any anthropologist entirely overlook a country's culture?

In Burundi those winter and summer months, I would sit in a small library in the capital and read the books and documents on *umuco* that I found there—they were written in Kirundi and French—and later I would discuss them with Uncle Nestor, an intellectual and far more knowledgeable than I about the culture and the Bashingantahe, and he would clarify things that puzzled me.

The nagging question for me, though, was one he couldn't answer: how to fix the political situation and end the unnecessary suffering that I had seen in most of the country, all of it the result of recurring civil unrest and the damage left by war. Perhaps this obsession was subconsciously fueled by my own experience during the war and by the fear I had felt when I was little. I remember a line from Plato: "We can easily forgive a child who is afraid of the dark; the real trag-edy of life is when men are afraid of the light." There are things that happen to you when you are little that never leave your psyche, and there is nothing as dis-turbing as the suffering of little children, especially when it is unnecessary. Some suffering may be neces-sary or at least inevitable, and one can derive a mean-ing from either type, but unnecessary suffering is a command to action. I remember reading Camus on rebellion and being moved by it. I wasn't contemplat-ing an armed invasion but an invasion of ideas, or what Camus called "a metaphysical revolt," which at its core, Camus explained, is a protest against evil. For me and for my country, this metaphysical revolt had to be the restoration of *umuco*—the light—and the Bashingantahe who embodied it. In the oath they took, they essentially agreed to be God's representa-tives on earth. In Kirundi, God can be a verb. He is also known as Jambo, "the Word." The missionary Bishop Julien Gorju had written that "the Burundian names for God are themselves alone a whole theod-icy." In Kirundi, *Kumana* means "to God" and *Ku-manira* "to God through." There is a Burundian saying, *Imana imanira mu bantu,* which means "God gods through people." If there is a way to defeat evil, in us and in the world, perhaps it is to allow God to god through us. During that period of my research, I believed that this could somehow be made to happen in my country, by bringing the Institution of Wisdom back to life.

When you are young, everything is possible, and you feel as if you are invincible. By the time I graduated from Williams, I was mostly disillusioned and was filled with regrets for having spent most of the past five years in Burundi, even when I was in America. Because I had been given the rich resources of a student in America, I had felt I should be able to fix the problems in my country and also in my family. I felt defeated. I was also exhausted.

Throughout my life, whenever I left home, Maman Clémence would have tears running down her cheeks. This continued. She cried each time I left to return to Williams. And then, during my sophomore year she came to visit us in America, first to Deo in Manhattan and then Asvelt and me in western Massachusetts. She stayed at the Kidders' house. Frances had created an elementary Kirundi dictionary on the table, with common nouns on one side and verbs on the other and connecting words between, so that she could ask Maman Clémence basic questions—did she want to eat, or was she tired or eager to go for a walk? They had a good time together, apparently. Maman Clémence went back home, and the next time I visited and was about to leave her again, she said goodbye in a very normal way, with no tears in sight. I never liked to see her cry, but I felt a little hurt. I said I was glad she wasn't crying this time, and she smiled and said, "So you're hurt that I no longer care about you." Then she explained that after she had spent a week with Frances and seen how well organized Williams was, and how beautiful its campus, she no longer worried about us but only missed us. Several years after I graduated from Williams, she came once again to America and spent a great deal of time with me in Brooklyn. She was quite ill. She died during a visit to grandchildren who had moved from Burundi to Canada.

By then I had all but given up on my dream of helping to reinstate the Bashingantahe in Burundi. And yet, more than once I found myself explaining the historical facts to strangers. There was for instance the day up in Maine when Kidder and I were returning from a boat ride, and he said that we were going to dinner that night with a distinguished medical anthropologist named Arthur Kleinman. He might be interested in the work in psychology I had done with Laurie, and indeed he was. In spite of my pessimism, I wondered if he might be willing to work with me on the Bashingantahe project. To my joyful surprise, the idea interested him too. Very much so, it seemed. He invited me to come see him in Cambridge, and Frances drove me there from Maine. I met Kleinman at the Harvard faculty club, and we spoke for more than two hours. It is strange how the idea of the Bashingantahe excites me, when it was their nature to be calm. I usually felt an adrenaline rush when I explained it. "We could work on this project and write books together, and we could recruit potential Bashingantahe and train them at Harvard," Dr. Kleinman was saying. He was very warm toward me: "Call me Arthur, and I will call you Paci." He gave me a tour of the Harvard campus and took me to the two buildings where he had offices, each in a different discipline. Clearly, he hadn't confined himself to a single place and subject. At last, I felt, my dream might be realized. The real question, Arthur said, was *how* to reintroduce those traditions of wisdom. But that was not a problem, I thought, because if we had the resources and expertise of Harvard, it would be like planting a garden. I thought, "culture," after all, comes from the verb "to cultivate." When we parted, he said, "Go write your book, and come back."

It took me a few years to finish this book. In the

meantime, I had another similar encounter. In following the news from Burundi, I had heard of a woman named Ketty Nivyabandi who had organized a large women's protest against the government's tyranny. She had been forced to flee Burundi and was trying to continue her protest in exile. I had read a poem of hers. In it, she writes of "men whose pettiness pierces the deep slumber of the ancients."

I contacted her by email and went to hear her speak at the United Nations in New York City. It was a fiery speech. I thought she would make a good president. Afterward we spoke for a time, and I found myself again talking about the Bashingantahe and saying it should be part of any solution to the problems she had described. She reacted strongly. I could see excitement in her face. She believed that if people were to hear about a plan for reviving that institution, they would demand that it be done. She said in effect that the memory of the Bashingantahe was still there, lying dormant. She conveyed this thought by looking down at the back of her hand and touching it with her fingernails, saying, "You only need to scratch."

Modern critics of the Bashingantahe, most of them radical Hutus who are in power, assert that the Institution of Wisdom "has always been the prerogative of the Tutsi and a few Hutus." Their argument is self-serving, but they may have a point. Some evidence suggests that over the centuries most Bashingantahe were Tutsi, and this suggests that the institution was biased in the way it recruited. That possibility troubles me. I would prefer to imagine that the Bashingantahe represented something close to moral perfection. Of course, that is childish fancy. What institution is without flaws?

I think an essential question is whether the Bashingantahe were biased in their actions. For a very long time Hutus have represented 85 percent of Burundi's population. A survey conducted just before the country's civil war found that well over 90 percent of *all* Burundians, Hutu and Tutsi, looked back with great respect, and even longing, to the Bashingantahe. Almost all the people surveyed said they wanted the institution revived, and after independence, efforts were in fact made to reconstitute it, but in a perverted form, like an ugly parody of its former self. I believe that if it had been truly reborn, as an instrument of peace, as a judicial system to which even kings had to yield, it would have neutralized the sources of our dreadful civil war. The war would have been impossible.

Instead of reviving a multiethnic Bashingantahe

institution, the radical Hutu government has created a civilian militia that the United Nations has condemned for waging "a campaign of fear and terror." This organization, which celebrates in chants the raping of women to increase its numbers, calls itself *imbonerakure*—"those who see from afar."

CHAPTER 7

Playing at Violence

"How could violence so easily be
turned into a game?"

On a fall afternoon, inside my dorm room at Deerfield Academy, I started hearing gunshots. I had been warned that in America people hunt with guns. I comforted myself with this thought at first, but the sounds went on and on and grew increasingly familiar. *It can't be hunting*, I thought. *People here don't hunt around school buildings, do they?*

I threw my door open and rushed outside the building, but I couldn't hear the sounds anymore. I saw students chatting and laughing as if everything was normal. Was I just dreaming? I went back inside the dorm. Walking down the hallway, I heard the sounds again. *Oh, it must be a student watching a movie!* I thought and returned to my room, closing the door. *Idiot!* I laughed at myself—where was I going to go anyway? I had just come to America, and I could hardly find my way around the campus. Even if the gunfire had been real, I would have had no idea where to run.

As I sat at my desk, the sounds brought back images from Kigutu. This disturbed me. Finally, I covered my ears. From time to time I would uncover them, hoping the movie had ended, but the sounds went on and on. *A movie of gunshots and nothing else? What type of movie is that?*

As dinnertime approached, students started emerging from their rooms, and I joined them in the hallway. "Were you just watching a movie?" I asked one of my dorm mates.

"Oh, I'm sorry! Was it loud?" he said.

"No, no!" I said. "I just was curious to know what movie you were watching."

"It wasn't actually a movie," he said. "I was playing video games."

Huh, I thought. I did not ask for an explanation. At the time, I didn't know what video games were, only that they made noises that sounded like gunfire.

There was a time when silence reigned all over my village. Rivers were loud, but their rhythmic sounds were part of the silence. People worked in their fields with hoes. There were no cars, no factories. I imagine that to Westerners that time and place would have resembled the Stone Age. Planes flew over the village, but never more than once a week. There was another season that broke this silence. It was the time of crops growing. From the early stage of the seeds' sprouting, parents would send their kids into the fields to make noise and chase away the birds that ate the seedlings. This went on for a month, and after that the silence would come again. I enjoyed the quiet, but it did not last. Another season erupted and broke all the silence. It was the season of war. It came in the fall when I was four, and it lasted for more than a decade.

In this new season, just as in any other, some things died and others were born. Everything was transformed. When the militia attacked a village, it left behind the remains of the dead—people and animals— and the houses in ruin. People moved from their houses to live in the forests. New words appeared— *ibinywamaraso* ("the blood drinkers") and *ivyamfurambi* ("deeds of the wrong firstborn")—and a new expression that meant "one after another, gently on a razor." This last slogan and others like it meant not to worry if you did not kill many people; the secret was to keep killing.

This new season made children my age wish they

had been born blind and deaf so they couldn't see their houses being burned and their mothers being raped before being killed, or hear the sounds of bombs or their parents screaming and crying. But at other times, you wished you had the eyes of a hawk and the ears of a deer, so that you could distinguish, in the dark, a black stump with branches from a man dressed in black pointing a gun, or a thin string tied to a mine from a long blade of grass lying across your path. These were times when you needed to know that the sound of raindrops falling on leaves wasn't that of militiamen approaching on tiptoe. For a while you wished for something, and after another while you wished for the opposite. You learned to cover your eyes in the day; you learned to see in the dark.

In the hallway at Deerfield, the boy, whom I'll call Luke, went on talking about video games as we waited for our classmates to join us for dinner. Almost everything Luke said was so confusing that I asked him: "What do you mean by saying you killed so-and-so?"

"Well, my enemies. Paci, how often do you play video games?"

"Actually, what are they?"

The other students looked at each other and smiled.

"Come on, Paci!" Luke led me to his room. He

took up a little device in his hands and turned on his computer. He pointed at the computer screen, at images of people with guns. "Once you press this button, they start moving, and you hunt them, see?" Out of the computer's speakers came the sound of shooting, the sound of war.

"You'll have to play with us, Paci!"

I faced the computer but lowered my eyes. I didn't want to offend him, but I didn't want to watch what was happening on the screen. Instead, I watched his fingers moving, handling the device.

"What are you doing with this thing?" I asked, pointing at the little device.

"I'm playing! That's how you play!"

"So you're actually doing the shooting?"

"Yeah! Here, you try it."

"No, no. Thanks. Let's go to dinner."

Before I enrolled at Buta, I spent a year at a public boarding school by the shore of Lake Tanganyika. This was in the seventh year of civil war. At that public school and many others, returning students hazed incoming ones. Although the rigor and form of hazing differed from one school to another, the objective of hazing was the same everywhere: to embarrass new students. Usually a group of returning boys and girls would gather in a circle around a new student, ordering him or her to tell vulgar jokes. This worked best with girls, who would often start crying halfway through a joke and be doubly embarrassed. Some new boys enjoyed telling dirty jokes, but all boys were embarrassed if they were made to cry in public, and if you were a boy, no matter how tough you were, you were unlikely to leave the center of the circle without wiping your eyes. Every word—every gesture—was treated as an insult by the hazers, and the penalty was for one of them to rap his knuckles on your head. If you were a girl, you often had to do more than tell a dirty joke. You might also be commanded by one of the boys, "Date me until I fall in love with you!" The hazers would tell you to caress the boy who had said those words. And then that boy would scream and call out, "She is harassing me! Please stop! Stop! Leave me alone! Leave me alone!" Other times the boy would make noises as if he were having sex and say things like, "What a whore!"

A person was assigned especially to haze me. His name was Chrysostom. Most of the hazers wanted to inflict only psychological pain. Chrysostom was different. If, for example, you saw a new girl cradling her breasts in pain, you knew that she had been hazed by Chrysostom.

I met him on my first day at that school. He came up to me and yelled, *"Kinyuzu!"* The name designated a new student who, according to the rules of hazing, did not deserve a proper name.

I did not reply.

"Why don't you open your mouth and say, 'Yes!' "

I kept quiet.

Chrysostom looked puzzled, as if I had done something not only incomprehensible but absolutely stupid. He then laughed ironically and called me by my proper name. "All right, Pacifique."

"Yes," I said.

"Are you surprised I know your name?" he asked.

"Well, yes, because we just met," I replied.

"Do you know my name?"

"No," I said.

"Because mine is too unimportant to know, but yours . . . You're a big shot, huh?"

Chrysostom was short but strong. He had a thick, muscular neck, and when he laughed, the muscles around his neck would get bigger and bigger as if air were being pumped into them. He was the boy who could get away with offending anyone, no matter how strong the other person was. Students would tell you: "Unless you intend to kill him, you should not try to fight Chrysostom." Whether you started the fight or he started it, it was for you to end it. You had to accept humiliation and ask for mercy. Otherwise the fight would never end. He would never quit.

From the moment we met until the end of the year, Chrysostom never let a day go by without spending some time with me. He made me his closest friend, in his special way of companionship. He always wanted me to tell him jokes, but he also made sure I did not go to sleep without being beaten up. Unlike others who often were not interested in jokes but only in inflicting humiliation, Chrysostom would listen to my jokes and would laugh when they amused him. If someone else had beaten me up, he did not need to beat me again. I only needed to go see him and tell him I had already been beaten, and then tell him jokes.

There was a particularly vulgar joke that hazers found funny, so new students told it often. The joke went like this: Two children are playing outside their house on a sunny afternoon. It is a hot day, and their parents are napping, windows wide open. All of a sudden, funny noises come out of their parents' room; they are making love. The boy runs over, looks through the window, and calls to his sister: "Mom and Dad are fighting!" The girl joins him at the window. After a while, they begin to cry. As they cry, the sister watches Mommy grabbing Daddy's shoulder and shouts, "Go, Mummy, go!" The brother grabs his sister, and a real fight begins—the kids are taking sides. After the parents have "come to peace," they hear their children fighting outside. They rush out and separate them and angrily question them, and the kids reply, *"But you were also fighting!"* This was the punch line.

When I told this idiotic joke to Chrysostom, he didn't laugh. After a moment of awkwardness, he asked me, "Were the kids *seriously* fighting?"

"The story goes that they fought to their bleed ing," I said. *Then* he burst into laughter. If there was anything related to violence in a joke, Chrysostom always wanted to hear more about it.

Another interesting thing about Chrysostom was that he wanted to tell *me* stories, too. He told me he lived in Bujumbura Rural, a province where a group of militia called the FNL (Forces nationales de libération) camped. He would tell me how he enjoyed watching the FNL combatants—whom he called friends—fighting with government soldiers. Though he never said that he himself killed or had fought for the FNL, in his stories he sometimes used "we." He would imitate the sounds of different guns and would keep doing it for such a long time that his voice would get hoarse. He repeated one story often. He never seemed to remember that I had already heard it. He laughed while telling it as if it were new every time.

"Back home, my friends, the FNL," he would start. "You know the FNL, right?"

I would nod.

"When we catch people . . . oh it is so funny . . . the soldiers . . . those for the government . . . oh dear! *Ntakintu kiryoshe nkico, wohora uraraba!* Nothing else on earth could be more amusing! You know how a cat, when he catches a mouse, you know how he can play with the mouse knowing that the mouse won't go anywhere? It is just like that. Oh, boy!" Then he would laugh and laugh. The muscles around his neck would swell. When he stopped laughing, he would go on: "We ask them questions, you know, and when they hesitate . . . You know, in the eyes!" He would stretch out his arm and aim his long fingernails at my eyes. "And then after—" He would interrupt himself with laughter again. "The FNL would never waste their bullets, you know, they would use a rope, you know, even a shoelace, and put it around their neck, and . . ." Saying this, he would grab my neck and squeeze it. "And . . . strangle the idiots!" Then, as if hit by an electric shock, he would release my neck and fall backward onto his bed, and laugh so hard that tears came from his eyes. "I miss home! I very much look forward to vacation." I could see he was absorbed by his story, as if he were right back there, strangling someone. He did not realize that I was shivering the whole time.

"What do *you* do on vacation?" he would ask me. For me, going on vacation did not mean going to my family's house, but rather joining my mother and brother in the forest, where we hid from Chrysostom's friends, the militiamen he always told me about. I could not tell him this, of course. I would change the subject.

I tried to please Chrysostom, hoping he would stop abusing me, but he was not aware of what I felt. I would take him to a restaurant, buy him soda and cookies, but it was like caressing a stone. He would often put his arm around my shoulders, and we would walk around while I told him jokes. He would listen very carefully and would laugh and even give me a high five. Students who saw us walking side by side thought we were the best of friends. In fact, Chrysostom himself seemed to think I was his best friend. When he learned I was going to another school for my remaining years of high school, he told me: "I will miss you! You are very sweet. I do not feel I will have someone else to spend time with and have fun." And I could see in his face that he actually meant it.

It was an interesting friendship, but I am glad that it ended.

That evening at Deerfield, on the way back from dinner, Luke asked me to play war video games with him. "No," I said. "I have a lot of work to do." I did have work to do. But I had other reasons for staying away. I thought that the boys who played the video games probably took drugs, that they were gangsters who pretended to be innocent.

One evening I was having trouble with my computer, and I went to Luke's room to ask him for help. I found him in the midst of shooting imaginary people. After he fixed my computer, he asked me if I wanted to watch him play for a little bit. I said I did not and tried to explain: "You know, I've seen the real thing. So I'm not really interested. I'm sorry."

"Wait, you . . . How?" He stopped playing.

"There was a war back in my country," I told him. "I was little when it started, and I grew up in it. So I saw a lot of that."

"Wow!" he said. He asked me to tell him more. There was excitement in his face, which surprised me, and frightened me a little. When I first came to school in America, I assumed that I would never talk about the war in Burundi. Doing so might refresh my bad memories. And wouldn't the other students think that I was violent myself? Besides, who would want to hear about such horrible things?

He wanted me to tell him about the war. I said I would tell him some other day, knowing that day would never come. It would have been like telling jokes to Chrysostom. Was this boy like Chrysostom? Was he addicted to violence, too? "And thanks so much for fixing my computer," I said and quietly left his room.

Over the next few months, I realized I was wrong about Luke. He and my other dorm mates who liked playing violent video games weren't gangsters at all. They were just young, inexperienced, innocent. It took me some time to realize that the shooting wasn't real to them. They were just playing. For them the games were "mindless," as one friend told me. Many kids at the school played the same kinds of games. So there was nothing unusual about Luke. He was just doing what many American kids did. I felt relieved, but I was also puzzled by what seemed to me like an odd sort of entertainment. How could violence so easily be turned into a game? How could companies invent such games in the first place? And how could parents buy them for their children?

Having lived through thirteen years of civil war, I know that violence can become almost a culture in itself, and that it twists not all but many of the people who are trapped in it. Of course, not all the children who grew up in the war became violent. How you responded to your own resentments, whether you seethed with thoughts of revenge, how your parents, neighbors, and friends responded to the bloodshed—all of these things helped determine your taste for violence. I was lucky. Many others were not. Maybe Chrysostom was a particularly sadistic case. I don't really know. Maybe he would have been a bad guy wherever he grew up. But he was not born violent, and certainly the war helped shape him. I don't know what happened to him as a child, but I imagine that since he grew up in that season of war in Burundi, he probably underwent a transformation and adapted the way a plant adapts. Violence in my country and in neighboring Rwanda and Congo had a similar effect on soldiers and militiamen, and especially on children drafted into armies or rebel militias. I remember how Nyandwi, a schoolmate and a neighbor who had joined one of the militias, hunted my family. When we escaped from him, he killed his own sister, apparently out of nothing more than frustration. I recall how Nyandwi, when he was no longer a militiaman, would proudly tell stories of how he killed thirty children with machetes in a single night. It was how his militia colleagues had initiated him, he explained.

I remember how Gilbert, a neighbor and Nyandwi's friend, enjoyed telling similar stories of when he was in the militia. How every one of his reactions, when he was back in the village, was violent, and how he always laughed after he had done something violent. How he would heat a nail and stab his sisters' feet to find out the truth if he suspected they had told him lies. To many young people, violence became easy and fun. It became one of their hobbies, as it seemed to have become Chrysostom's hobby. It is hard to allow yourself to imagine that you could become one of those young people, but you have to admit that you could when you remind yourself that the children who are twisted by war were once lovely three-year-olds who smiled and charmed with their innocence.

I think back to the season of war and remember how we fled deep into the jungle, far from any people. That was how we managed to survive, by hiding, by turning our backs on the rest of humanity. Those parents who sent their children into the jungle to protect them from the bloodshed—they would have envied the peace that Luke and others like him took for granted. Most of all, they would have envied the fact that these lucky children did not know the true devastation of war. That they only played at violence.

The Saga of the Watusi

"When I felt tears streaming down, I wiped
my eyes and repeated to myself what I
had heard the adults say: that the
tears of a man flow inward."

One day in late spring, after I had been gazing out my window in Brooklyn and feeling homesick, I closed the curtain and picked up a book, *Sightings of the Sacred.* It contained beautiful photographs of cows and bulls, including the Cattle of Kings—such elegant horns! Looking at these pictures only made me more nostalgic. I found another book, *Cattle of the Ages,* coauthored by the same photographer and by the president of South Africa who had recently brought the Cattle of Kings to his own country. He had also written a memoir about his encounters with my family's kind of cattle and his fondness for them. When I came across an article titled "The Cattle of Kings Surface in America," I wondered, *Could our cows be here?* I read the article openmouthed. *Yampaye inka we!* God who gave me cows! Our cows were indeed here. In America. In fact, there were some in upstate New York, only a few hours away from my apartment. A married couple, Julie and Tom Markert, kept some Cattle of Kings on their farm in a town called Downsville. I emailed Julie to schedule a visit.

I went back to my window, opened the curtain, and gazed at the horizon, beyond the hills of Staten Island. Soon, I thought, I will be seeing my friends again, on some mountain meadow, somewhere over there.

I left Brooklyn on a Saturday early morning. It seemed straightforward to simply cross the Verrazano Bridge, right next to my apartment, and head north. But I followed my GPS and took a roundabout route to the Brooklyn-Queens Expressway, and then around Manhattan and through the Lincoln Tunnel. More than once I found myself at a standstill in long lines of cars. It was hard to relax in the traffic, so I played some folk music from home—a CD of love songs to cows.

Playing this music had always made me feel homesick, but this time it felt like homecoming. As I drove, I grew increasingly excited at the prospect of seeing my old companions. I stopped a few hours later at a place I had read about called the Catskill Game Farm. I had learned that this had been the first and largest privately owned zoo in the United States, and also the first to import my family's kind of cattle. But it was no longer operating as a zoo; the place was being renovated. I went straight to the African section, where the cattle had been kept. It was empty. Yet to have arrived on this site where they had been was close enough to keep me going. It was getting late but I was determined to find my old companions. I ate a sandwich in the car and then drove on to Downsville. My GPS stopped working on the way, and I got lost. I saw a man working in a graveyard, and I pulled over and asked for directions. He was friendly. I had missed just one turn, and I was only about thirty minutes away. So far there had been thick woods and no meadow or farm in sight. But as I entered Downsville, I saw a mountain meadow on my left, and my eyes began darting. My guardian angel must have taken over my steering wheel. In no time, I spotted my friends by their majestic horns. *There, there they were, my old pals!* Grazing peacefully right below the mountain meadow. I felt an urge to drive fast, the kind of urge you feel when you want to run and hug a friend you haven't seen for a long time.

There was a parking lot in the valley just below the mountain meadow, right across from Downsville Central School. I parked in front of the school, got out, and stood staring at the cattle grazing in the meadow that rose in front of me. I gazed long enough to quench the longing I felt in front of my window in Brooklyn. Then I heard a woman's voice behind me.

"Are you lost?" she asked.

"I am home," I said quietly to myself and then turned toward the voice and asked the woman where Julie and Tom lived.

She gave me directions to the restaurant they owned. "Old Schoolhouse" read the sign outside. In the lobby, on a wall, hung a pair of giant horns. From my reading online I had learned you could buy a pair like this mounted on an acrylic base, but it cost nearly two thousand dollars. I looked up at the horns for a while and then went inside the restaurant and asked for Julie. She appeared in jeans and a white shirt. "So, you want to see the Watusi?" she asked.

Some people call the Cattle of Kings the Watusi. I told her I had already seen them and was here to ask if I could go to the barn to see the small ones.

"If you go to the barn," Julie said, "they will come up to you and lick your hands, and there's one that's really friendly."

We chatted for a while. "So where is home for you now?"

"Brooklyn, New York," I said.

"Wow, you drove a long way. Just driving to check them out and then driving back home?"

"Yes," I said, and started explaining that I grew up with these cattle and that they were in many ways part of my family. "I am a Tutsi," I said. "And my people, back then they called us Watusi. So the cattle actually carry the name of my people."

"Is that right?" Julie said. She seemed genuinely surprised.

I asked her how she and her husband had come to purchase these cattle.

"A gentleman lived up the road," she said. "His name was Mister Finney. He had a Watusi bull." Julie took me back into the lobby and pointed to the horns mounted high on the wall. "That Watusi bull," she said. "The bull's name was Catskill Thunder, and he was from the Catskill Game Farm. Mister Finney got rid of his cattle. He knew that my husband had cows, so he called him up and said, 'I'll give you this bull if you'll take care of him and let him die on the farm. Just feed him, take care of him.' My husband said okay. So they went and loaded this great huge Watusi bull, and brought him over there." She pointed to the mountain meadow. "And *everybody* was just *amazed* by the size of the bull and the horns he had. Then my husband bought some heifers from the

Catskill Game Farm and started breeding them. We had a lot more heifers than we do now."

Julie started sharing cow stories with me. One was about a small Watusi bull that had been born here on the farm. "I named him Comanche. This *really cool* name, you know. And then this southern man came down a few weeks later to buy a pair of Watusi cattle, and he says, 'How much for that little bull?' And my husband says, 'Well, I'll have to ask my wife.' You know, because he really didn't want to sell him. So we put a high price on him, and the guy bought him anyway, and the bull ended up being this magnificent animal. He was *dog gentle,* you know, you'd pat him, he'd follow you on a leash, and we sold him. We should never have done that!"

I thought of course about my grandfather and how he could never sell a cow, and about Bigeni, whom my father had treacherously sold out from under me. It is a remarkable thing, how you can truly be a stranger in a strange land and suddenly find yourself in the presence of someone who makes you think *We understand each other perfectly.*

Feeling more at home than I had in a long time, I went back inside the restaurant with Julie and took a photo of the Watusi horns at the entrance.

"I am glad you could find us," Julie said, "and had a chance to come up."

"What's the name of that mountain?" I asked, pointing to the mountain meadow.

"There's really no name on it. It's my husband's." And then she named it, laughing, "Tom's Mountain."

I thanked Julie, and as I waved goodbye to her, I saw Tom in a utility vehicle across the street, signaling me to follow him to the ranch. We parked in front of his barn. A big banner on the front of it bore an inscription that read, "Farmers for Trump. Make America Great Again."

Tom and I shook hands, and then we went inside to see the heifers. It was a little wet in there, but Tom had work boots on, and he went in to bring me the heifers while I stood at the gated door. He grabbed each by the horns and brought them to me one by one, rubbing their necks while I looked at them.

"How old is that one?" I asked.

"Oh, a year and a half." She already had big horns. I made a herding whistle, the kind of sound I used to make when I took my family's cattle to pasture in the morning and when I called them home from the mountain meadows. It was the same sound that often accompanied our pastoral poems and love songs to cows. The heifer came to me and licked my hand. I chatted with Tom for a while. He said I could buy Watusi cows online if I wanted, and he had one of his heifers on sale. I didn't tell him that I had no land, no place for a cow, but I thanked him for his time and went to take another look at the big ones grazing on the mountain meadow. I asked Tom to take a picture of me with my phone while I stood near the Cattle of Kings, and then we said good-bye.

I took one more look at the meadow and then turned and stared for a moment at the banner on Tom's barn— "Farmers for Trump. Make America Great Again." I thought of the warm exchange I'd just had with Julie and the laughter we had shared talking about cows, and also of Tom's generosity—stopping work and taking me to his barn—and I felt unsure how to reconcile these inter-actions with the news and political campaigning that were dominating the media here in the United States. I felt a sad cognitive dissonance. What I'd heard on the news and from American friends had made me think that I wouldn't—and shouldn't—feel comfortable among people who had voted for Trump. We would have noth-ing in common, I had assumed. Now I thought about the identity politics in my native country and I told myself, *It's all the same.* I pushed those thoughts away and thought about cows instead, as I often did as a little boy during the war in my country. Back then, I liked to turn my mind to our cows for the simple reason that I loved them. I was also drawn by the tranquility I felt watching them graze in the green meadows. I now realize that this had the effect of meditation; it was another way to escape from thinking about war. I associated the Cattle of Kings with an era of peace and abundance in my country, which I grew up hearing about from folks and their folklore. People of that time, I was told, were concerned with living virtuous lives, in harmony with nature. They had strict dietary rules. It was forbidden to combine meat and milk, for instance, especially among the Tutsi. My family had observed this rule, and I always used to choose milk over meat.

Every time I heard the old stories and pastoral poems and love songs to cows, I felt I wanted to live in that country, and whenever I was with cows I felt I had been transported to the deep past of the Country of Milk and Honey. As I was growing up in Burundi, I started to miss this country that I knew only from folklore, as if I were living in exile in some other country far away from home—the country of war. My wish as a little boy had been to see this peaceful country again. Now, a decade after I had left Burundi, as I drove away from Tom's barn I found myself thinking that if I had made public my wish as a little boy, I would have hung a banner similar to Tom's in the same spot, but with the inscription "Lord,

Make Burundi a Country of Milk and Honey Again." There would have been no better spot to hang my banner than on Tom's barn, because the cattle inside were for me a living memory of that bygone era in which I was living in my mind.

Back in Burundi, when I was a teenager there had been no candidate that I would have voted for. The campaigning had been a politics of division, which had led to war. I hadn't understood much of anything then. But I remember that when I was little, I went to church often, to pray that war would end. There was a prophetic lyric that the choir often sang. It spoke of a messiah's returning. The sign would be a trumpet's blowing that would make the earth tremble. The part about the trumpet made me think of cows and their long horns from which people made trumpets in the time of kings. In my mind, the return of this king of the earth and the heavens would end the war and restore my country. When I took my grandpa's cows to pasture, in the land of sorghum to which we had fled, I often found myself singing this sad and soothing song. When I felt tears streaming down, I wiped my eyes and repeated to myself what I had heard the adults say: that the tears of a man flow inward. I tried to learn how not to cry by using a technique I had heard the grown-ups describe when they advised you to "bite your heart," a metaphor I applied literally, by pressing my teeth together. When it worked I could comfort myself that I was not a sad and scared little boy, and had succeeded at making my tears flow inward like a man.

I had seen the tears of a cow flow outward and realized that our cows also cried, in silence. But I had never seen the tears of a bull, and I think that is why the adults also advised you to have the heart of a bull. For a long time I wished I could develop one of those, but my heart felt too soft and melted too easily, and the only technique that worked for me was to be on guard, always ready to clamp my teeth together as if I were literally biting my heart.

I knew that cows could be frightened, because I saw them get startled. Bulls were artful in responding to fear. I never saw one flinch, not even at thunder, which terrified our herding dog, Rurebeya, but aroused the bull to roar back, as if to threaten the thunder in turn, bellowing so ferociously that the sound echoed across the mountain meadows. When lightning and thunder struck, the bull and the shepherd worked in unison to counter the threat from the sky. It was the custom for a shepherd to beat the ground with a baton while saying *"Humura! Humura!"* (Fear not!) Meanwhile, the bull would lower its head and gouge a hole in the earth with its horns and hooves. While beating the ground, the shepherd also made a high-pitched sound. The bull followed the same pattern. It dug and roared at the ground, then raised its head and roared at the thunder. I remember performing the shepherd's rite as a little boy and feeling scared by the thunder but finding reassurance in the bull's roar.

My mother had told me a story about lightning striking some of the cattle of my grandfather's cousin. They had been grazing on a meadowland in a valley, some distance below another meadow called the Boys' Hill where my parents' cattle were grazing. There was no bull in the cousin's herd but my parents had a big one. When the lightning struck, my parents' bull came down from the Boy's Hill roaring, roaring into the valley, where several cattle lay motionless on the grass. My mother was home at this time. She remembered hearing a deafening roar, and immediately she thought of the cows. She took a baton and went to check on the cattle grazing in the pasture on the Boy's Hill. She had to descend to the valley and then climb up the other side. In the valley she stumbled upon the stricken cattle and trembled at the sight of the apparently lifeless cows. There was a distinct and terrible odor that smelled, she said, "like burnt horns." She retreated and took a roundabout route to the Boy's Hill. On her way up, she met my parents' bull coming down. The bull advanced, sniffing the air every few steps and roaring. She called the bull by his name and tried to sweet-talk him into retreating, trying to direct him with her baton. In ordinary times the bull and the cattle obeyed her, but this situation was different, and it was grave. A roar had thundered down from the sky and on cue the bull had roared back at the thunder, but he could sniff death in the air, and he was on a rescue mission, determined to wake up the stricken cattle in the valley. He paid no heed to my mother's calming voice and motioning baton but advanced in my mother's direction, down toward the valley, roaring ferociously, sniffing the air, digging with his horns and hooves, and roaring again. My mother was scared and got out of his way, following him. When the bull finally arrived and saw the stricken cattle, thrown down and lifeless, he roared with rage. He roared and roared and roared, trying to wake up his cows. Five of them heeded the bull's roar and stood up. Several others were dead.

When lightning killed a cow, it was forbidden to say that the thunder had struck. You said that the thunder "gave." It was a euphemism accompanied by a custom—whoever lost cows to lightning received cows from family members, friends, and neighbors. That evening, my grandfather's cousin received three cows. They came from my grandfather, from a neighbor, and from a friend.

In the old times, my people prayed beneath the tree of God before a journey. Journeying was a constant theme in their folklore: "*Nzogenda*, I shall go" was a lyric in their songs, and "May you go forth" was a common blessing. I now realize that our cows have even joined us where we are scattered across the four continents, as if they were also part of the diaspora and the folkloric journeying. After my trip to the Watusi in upstate New York, I read an article titled "The Saga of the Watusi Cattle" and was able to trace on my globe the journey they made by sea from the port of Mombasa, in Kenya. There they were loaded onto a cargo ship and traveled the Indian Ocean along the eastern coast of Africa, north into the Gulf of Aden, and continued northwest up the Red Sea through the Suez Canal, and then traveled the Mediterranean Sea west, through the Straits of Gibraltar, and finally north, through the English Channel to Hamburg, Germany, where they were kept in the zoo in Leipzig. From Germany, these cattle spread throughout Europe to Sweden, England, and Denmark. Finally, from Europe they were exported to Australia and Canada, and finally to the United States.

CHAPTER 8

By the Fire

"Writing it, I felt as if I had my hands
on the memory."

After I graduated from Williams, I went back to
Burundi and spent an indolent summer with my
friend Fabrice from Buta, touring the hills of the
country, including those of Gihinga, where Maman
Clémence was born. I returned to the States toward
the end of the summer. I had applied to study public
health at Columbia and had been offered a scholarship, although I didn't enroll. An article of mine had
been published in *The American Scholar,* and someone who read it offered me a contract to write a book,
but I didn't respond: writing that piece had been painful, whereas writing for myself—that is, writing without feeling that I was doing it for publication—had
always felt pleasant, even therapeutic. I didn't tell
Kidder about the offer I had received because I was

afraid he would encourage me, and it would have been hard to say no.

I had resisted taking writing courses at Williams, but I enjoyed talking writing with Kidder. Looking back now, I feel as if after Williams, I went to *his* school. We discussed writing, and I talked to him often about the Bashingantahe, which he said he found fascinating. I reasoned that writing a book might be one way to pursue my dream that I might live to see the Bashingantahe re-created in Burundi. Besides, I no longer knew what to do with my life. So I wrote a book proposal based on a story I had written for myself five years before at the Kidders' summer house in Maine. I rewrote it and Kidder edited it, and I received a contract from Random House, which I welcomed now that I had a goal in mind.

As I wrote, I began studying the Bashingantahe again, rereading all the material I had gathered and trying to bring it back to life in my own mind. As I studied, I discussed my ideas with Kidder. At one point, I went to Maine alone and stayed there for four months, writing and thinking. I bought a flip phone and disconnected myself from the internet. Gradually, as I wrote, I began feeling haunted by regrets again. This project was another naïve undertaking, I felt, causing me more pain for nothing. But Kidder kept encouraging me, and I enjoyed his company.

When I returned to western Massachusetts, he and I often went mountain biking. I remember riding with him in the woods, always in the afternoons, after our writing hours. Most of the trails we rode were only a few miles from his house, but they went up and down and around the hills, and along old roads bordered by stone walls, sometimes as far as twenty miles. We gave our routes names, "Broken Chain," "Nightmare in the Mud," "Fell on the Ice." He liked keeping a record of the rides he took, and the ones we rode together when I was staying with him amounted to something like three thousand miles. As we rode, he told me stories and histories of these old trails through the woods and beside streams and rivers. Other times he talked to me about writing. Nature's sights and sounds—trees, birds—reminded him of some of his favorite poems on nature: Robert Frost's *Birches*, for instance, or John Keats's *Ode to a Nightingale*, which he would recite. I remember riding with him through Boston's Arnold Arboretum, which Frances called "a museum of trees." I remember a spring day when the astonishing sight of the arboretum's cherry trees in bloom made us stop, and Kidder said: "Loveliest of trees, the cherry now is hung with bloom along the bough." I thought this was his own spontaneous observation, but of course I later learned the lines came from a poem by A. E. Housman.

I think Kidder recited poems to quiet his active mind. Sometimes he used poetry as a sleeping pill. When he went to bed or woke up in the middle of the night, he would recite poems and put himself back to sleep that way. In Burundi, there is a fancy saying that to go to sleep is to anoint your eyes with oil. Kidder anointed his with poems. On winter nights, the Kidders and I often sat talking beside their fireplace. It was my self-appointed job to light the fire and keep it going.

"It's a beautiful fire," he'd exclaim, as he sat in the living room, now lit with the fire's glow.

He'd stare at the fire and call to Frances, "Frannie, come see the fire!" He would say this with a certain innocence, which we all shared, like little boys and girls.

I had brought a small chair from Burundi, a type called *songa bugari*. It was small and just wide enough for your derriere. I could place it right next to the fire. When I positioned myself there, I knew I would soon be treated to a poem or a story or just a fun discussion. Sometimes we argued over ideas. My favorite memory is when he'd make rules—"We mustn't be mad at each other!"—or when he'd say, "Shut up, shut up, I understand what you're saying now," and then get up and go the kitchen, saying, "Let me pour myself a glass of wine." And then he would come back and speak from the depths of his wisdom and intellect, drawing from a distilled life's experience of writing and reading. I sat and listened, trying to absorb every one of his words. When he was done, he'd turn again to the glowing fire, and soon you'd hear a poem. I remember one night when he recited Shakespeare's sonnet that contains these lines:

In me thou see'st the glowing of such fire,
That on the ashes of his youth doth lie,
As the death-bed, whereon it must expire,
Consumed with that which it was nourish'd by.

I liked to watch his mouth, the way he savored words as if he were savoring food. He liked to tease me. He'd accuse me of stealing his sandals, which their dog used to do. Sometimes I teased him back, and when I was lucky, I could find a perfect tease. The time for instance after he had recited that Shakespeare sonnet and then, noticing that the fire was dying, yelled, "Paci, what happened to the fire?"

"Consumed with that which it was nourished by," I said.

He laughed. "Touché."

I recall these moments with great fondness. They reminded me of similar moments in my childhood during the times of stories, when children listened to elders while seated around a fire outdoors and more often around an indoor fireplace—usually constructed on the floor in the middle of a room. The storytellers were very pleasant. I remember one we children called *Sogo*, short for "Grandfather." Sitting with Kidder around the fire and listening to him talk about books or poems or stories felt like listening to the good storytellers I was fond of when I was little. It was as if I had found again my Sogo, but in *iburaya*—far away.

Writing, of course, was different from listening to stories, and not always pleasant. I remember Kidder quoting John Milton, saying, "The mind is its own place, and in itself can make a heaven of hell, a hell of heaven." I remember him also telling me: "Art has the great power to transform the experience of suffering and injustice into something beautiful."

The first time I wrote a story about a dreadful memory from the war, I actually felt relieved. I could control the experience. If it was only in my mind, I could not. Writing it, I felt as if I had my hands on the memory and could control it and try to make it beautiful. So instead of its having power over me, I had power over it. When a bad memory intruded on my peace, it dictated my feelings. But when I first began writing from my memories, I could remember what had happened without the old bad feelings. I would think of some modification of the story that would make the story better. When I first started writing, if a memory woke me up I could get back to sleep by writing it down, hoping I could turn it into something beautifully written.

The Times of Stories

"I experienced art before I knew the word."

When I was little, I used to climb trees, and from their tops I would gaze in all directions trying to see the end of my country. I was sure that, like the moon, my country was a big chunk of land surrounded by nothing but air. How terrifying it must be, I thought, to come to the border of my country. Sometimes I dreamed that I came to the edge, and I woke up just before I fell off.

My parents' house sat on a plateau. From there you could look down to the west and see the lowlands and then a huge lake and at the other side of the lake, the Ubwari Peninsula of Zaire, the current Congo. I knew that like a river the lake had land beneath it, and that land connected the place where I lived to the Ubwari Peninsula. So there wasn't a real separation, not an edge I could fall from. Often people would point at the peninsula and say, "That's Zaire." The fact that it had another name did not matter. For me, it was another piece of land that belonged to my country, Burundi.

Little by little, I learned names such as Rwanda and Tanzania, and I came to accept them as different countries. But Burundi was certainly the main one, the most important of them. Zaire, Rwanda, and Tanzania were just a tiny elongated piece of land that surrounded my country.

At that time, when I was little, Burundi had many wild animals. There were elephants and leopards in the valley of the Rusizi River, hippos and crocodiles in the lake next to where I lived, and monkeys, baboons, and gorillas in my home village. A canyon next to my parents' house was called Nyentambwe, "a place of lions." I had not yet run into one of those. All these animals were frightening, but the most frightening animal to me wasn't wild but domestic. It was a pig.

In my home village I grew up hearing the tale of a pig that escaped a butchering and then started running after people, eating them. Men threw spears at it but missed. For several days villagers could not go outside their compounds because they feared the raging pig. One version of the tale said the pig was finally captured and killed. Another version said the pig went into the forest and became wild. There were also tales of pigs eating their own babies, and even small children, when they were hungry. My siblings told me this when I was little, just to scare me so I wouldn't go wandering alone down the dirt road beside our house. Because of the tales I had heard, I would freeze at the sight or sound of a pig. Even though I often saw little kids my age playing near them, I imagined that pigs were very unpredictable and might eat me anytime.

But there were more interesting and less frightening stories than the ones about pigs. Elderly people told a lot of stories. All of them led, or were supposed to lead, to a moral lesson. Some stories were fables, which often made reference to animals, and elders made it clear that these stories were fictional. As a rule, fables were told only at night, usually indoors around the fire. And then there were stories in which characters were people. Most of these stories were also fictional, but the elders always claimed they were true. The "true" stories could be told anytime, but for convenience they were often told in evenings, when day work was finished and everyone was seated inside by the fire.

In those days, most people in villages had round houses made of wood and mud with thatched roofs, and inside the house there was a rounded fireplace built of clay. It had the shape of an inflated tire and was called *urubumbiro*. Around the fireplace there were usually traditional handwoven mats on which children would lie or sit, waiting for dinner or bedtime or stories. It was a tradition in Burundi for elders to tell stories to children, and so in most households every evening was story time.

Some elders were particularly good at telling stories, and they were usually known for this beyond the household—called "the good storyteller," for instance, or "the funny old man." These elders were like magnets to children. The way they told stories was more important than the stories themselves. You might have already heard a story that bored you, but when these elders repeated it you would be kicking your legs up and pedaling your feet, laughing. The good storytellers could do more than make you laugh. Sometimes a story would become more and more puzzling as they told it, and you would still be waiting for a revelation when the story ended. The elders seemed to enjoy this effect. They also told sad stories that made my eyes well up with tears. Sad stories often began with "In the old days" or "When I was young" or "Before you were born" or "It used to be." If a story began with the phrase *Harabaye, ntihakabe*

("There once was, there shall never be"), you sensed that the story was going to be fictional.

What was it about these elders who could transform a story that was boring into something amusing and intriguing, even moving? I think it was the tone of their voices and the gestures they made with their hands, and the suspense they created by reordering the stories. And they surprised you with the words they chose. Sometimes they made people and places so vivid you thought those fictional characters were real. All these things dressed up a story, transformed it, and made it a beautiful tale. Now I realize that as a child, I experienced *art* before I knew the word.

I did not hear stories from my grandparents. My family had moved far away from them, to a different part of the country. My mother told stories, and so did my father when he was drunk. But I preferred listening to the elderly people who visited us once in a while, relatives or neighbor friends of my parents.

One afternoon my father sent me to an elderly man named Ntasoni to fetch some ibondo, a liquid used to prepare wine. Ntasoni lived on a hill far from my home, about six miles away. Small children were often sent on errands, and six miles wasn't a great distance in a place where everyone walked everywhere. But I was only four. I had not yet begun school, and it was the first time I had been asked to go that far by myself. I was afraid of meeting animals on my way but also eager for the adventure. My mother and father had argued about letting me go alone. My mother worried about me.

I had to climb a hill to reach Ntasoni's little house. When I got there I saw the place had a very nice view. From the front door you could see boats far below on the lake. In the other direction you could see cars on the road that crossed the mountain named Honga. Ntasoni was sitting on a bamboo chair outside the door. He had a wispy gray beard and a merry face. I think he might have been in his eighties, but to me he was just old.

"I would live here forever!" I told him when I arrived.

"What do you like here that you don't have at your home, my little one?"

"From home, I can't watch cars driving on Honga."

"You come here then, and live with me," he said.

"If I come, will you tell me fables?"

"Oh, yes! I have a lot of them."

"Do you have one for me now?"

But he would not break the custom. "No, we don't tell fables in the day. We only tell them in the night."

I gazed back at the mountain road and the cars,

which were small in the distance. "I like cars! Do you know where you can find one?"

"Cars are made in Iburaya," he said.

"Where is that?" I asked. "I would like to go there sometime and get a car!"

"It is very far away, my little one! Iburaya is where muzungus live. They are the ones who make cars. They also make bicycles, motorcycles, planes, and all sorts of complicated things."

"Who are muzungus?" I asked.

"They are different people," he replied. He added, "They look like pigs!"

"I hate pigs!" I exclaimed. "I am very afraid of them!"

"So you do not want to go to Iburaya!" He was howling with laughter.

"Didn't you say they are people?"

"Yes, people who look like pigs." He was still laughing hard. "You are such a lovely kid! Take the Ibondo home. It is getting late, and when you come back, I will tell you more."

I didn't know it then, but the words "Iburaya" and "muzungu" that I had just learned from Ntasoni described a whole new world, and a whole new people. Originally, Iburaya referred to Germany and Belgium, the two countries that had colonized Burundi. But by the time I was born, at least for rural people, Iburaya meant anywhere far away from Burundi. As for muzungu, it too once meant Germans or Belgians, but it had come to include everyone who was white or anyone of any color who was rich. When Ntasoni told me that muzungus were people who looked like pigs, he meant to insult Burundi's former colonial masters. At the time I took his words literally and imagined an actual resemblance between muzungus and pigs. I had heard one fable about a king with ears as long as those of a cow and another about creatures that were part human and part animal. With muzungus, my imagination had free rein. I imagined all sorts of things. None of them had a human form. Whatever a muzungu is, I thought, it must be ugly and terrifying.

I returned home with many questions and found my father sitting on his bamboo chair in front of the house. I handed him the bottle of Ibondo. He smelled it and put it down. Maybe it was good or maybe it wasn't, he didn't say. Nevertheless, I sat down near him, hoping he would say "Good kid!" He didn't.

"Papa, Ntasoni told me things I did not understand!"

My father kept quiet.

"Papa, have you seen people who look like pigs?"

He yelled, "Is that why you were late? Have you

been talking to Ntasoni all the afternoon?" He told me to leave him alone and go see Maman, and that I had better not say things I heard at other people's houses or he would punish me. He had a bad temper, and I was very late. Maybe my mother had been fretting and blaming him for sending me on that errand.

A few days after visiting Ntasoni, I went down to the river with my brother Asvelt and sister Daphrose to fetch water. We were on the way back when I heard my brother cry out, "Look! A muzungu!" I looked up and saw a strange but not entirely unfamiliar-looking creature coming in our direction. It looked nothing like a pig. It looked like a man. He was very tall, but everyone was tall to me. His skin was white. He had strange hair—straight and so long that it fell down his back, like hay on his shirt. Although my siblings seemed happy to see the muzungu, I was very scared. Perhaps because it was my first encounter with this kind of person, perhaps because the word "muzungu" triggered grotesque images, or perhaps the combination of these things, I ran back toward the river and hid in a bushy spot by the road. As I ran, I heard my siblings laughing at me.

Hidden in the bush, I started calming down. If my siblings were excited to see the muzungu and were laughing at me for running, there was nothing dangerous after all. I wondered, though, why Ntasoni had said muzungus looked like pigs. I had just discovered that it wasn't true. After the muzungu walked on and was out of sight, I emerged from my hideout and ran after my siblings. They were still laughing at me, and I was embarrassed, but I never told anyone what I had heard from Ntasoni. I wanted badly to see him again, but it seemed impossible because Maman had told me never to go to Ntasoni's house again—it was too far for a child my age.

Maybe I could find a way, though. When my father used up the Ibondo, maybe he would send me to Ntasoni again. But when I checked I saw that the bottle was still full. Finally, one morning he placed the bottle on his worktable, which meant he was going to use the Ibondo that day. It happened that my mother wasn't home. This was the perfect time, I thought, for me to visit Ntasoni.

My father went to his room and left the Ibondo on the table. Our cat was sitting on a chair next to the table. I tiptoed slowly across the dirt floor and lifted the cat onto the table. I poured the liquid on the floor, dropped the empty bottle, and yelled so my father would hear "*Ohh!* Papa will kill you!"

"What's wrong?" my father yelled from his room.

"Yabu!" I replied. Yabu was the cat.

"Did she knock over my Ibondo?" my father yelled again.

"Yes!" I replied.

My father strode out of his room and hit the cat. Too bad! But I did not like that cat anyway; she used to drink my milk.

My father was saying he needed the Ibondo that day. I said, "Papa, I can run fast to Ntasoni's house and get you more!"

"I would give you a present!" he replied.

"You don't need to!" I said to myself.

Quick as a rabbit, I took the bottle and headed toward Ntasoni's. Maybe he would do as he promised and tell me a story, but I also wanted to ask him why he had said that muzungus look like pigs. I ran all the way so I would have time for this conversation. I arrived breathing hard.

"Does your father already want another Ibondo?" Ntasoni asked.

"Yes."

"He must make a lot of wine!"

"Yes, he drinks a lot," I replied. "So, Grandpa, tell me more."

"Tell you more about what?"

"About the pigs."

"Didn't you tell me you hate pigs?" He started laughing again.

"Grandpa, I met a muzungu. He was a man and he did not look like a pig!"

"You must have met a wrong one!" he told me, still laughing. "And I think I know who you met. Those are called Swedes. They are working with a local church."

"Grandpa, my siblings called him muzungu when we met him!"

He lit a cigarette and said, "Come sit closer to me."

I sat on the ground beside his chair and he started to explain. "The people we called pigs, my little one, were the first muzungus. They weren't good people. Before the muzungus, we had our own *umwami*—the king. He reigned all over Burundi, and we lived peacefully. Then the muzungus invaded our country. The king resisted, but muzungus had powerful weapons. They didn't need to even get close to you. They would kill you from a distance. They killed many, many, many people! And then they burned the kingdom and ruled the country. The first who arrived were the Germans. They were cruel. But then came their cousins the Belgians, and they were even crueler. If you had chickens, you had to take the eggs to muzungus; you weren't allowed to eat them. When you had a nice sleek cow, they would tell you to kill it and give them meat."

"Oh! They were very bad!" I said, interrupting him. I already loved cows.

"You see that road, my little one?" He pointed at the road that climbed across Honga. "I worked on it. Belgians would be standing with their guns and batons while we would be digging into the mountain. As you see, it is very steep, and when the earth loosened above you, it could slide down and bury you alive. You couldn't stop digging even when you were tired. If you became too exhausted to move, the Belgians would hit you with a baton and throw you down the hill, and while you lay there the men would continue to shovel dirt and it would cover you. Many died."

Ntasoni lit another cigarette. He wasn't laughing anymore.

"Germans were smarter than Belgians," he continued. "They didn't stay as long as the Belgians did, but they brought advanced things to our country. The Belgians, however, took more from us than they brought us. Many people wish the Germans had stayed longer. But no one knows if they were developing the country for us. They probably thought they were developing it for themselves. They had a very big, big plan! There was a war all over the world, my little one! The Germans were not only cruel to us, they also invaded other countries in Iburaya. They wanted to conquer the world but they lost the war, and that's how the Belgians came to replace them. The Belgians stayed for a very long time and left hatred among our people. Before, we were one people, but now, my little one, you will hear people call themselves this and that."

He talked and talked, he couldn't stop. I told him I had to leave and take the Ibondo home. It was getting late.

From Ntasoni's account, Iburaya—Europe—was a place where complicated things came from: cars that ran like the wind, planes that flew over the land like birds, and all sorts of other complicated things. The people who lived there were called muzungus. They weren't pigs, but they weren't good, either. To kill a sleek cow! And hit people and put them under the soil!

He had not explained how the Swedes were different from Germans or Belgians. But they were called muzungus, too, and they also lived in Iburaya. I went back home with more questions than I had brought.

· · ·

I planned to play another trick and go back to see Ntasoni, but in October of that year, when I was nearly five years old, the civil war broke out. It lasted for the next thirteen years, and I never saw Ntasoni again.

My understanding of the world had been growing, but the war made everything confusing. I had been asking questions about every little thing, but now I asked them not out of curiosity but out of fear and confusion. Before, if you had asked an adult why people die, or if you had asked, "Am *I* going to die?" you would have been told that a time comes when God calls you and you go to live with him in heaven, and this would have been said in a tone that made dying seem something not to worry about because it was not imminent. But now, those children's questions were no longer answered with ease. They were not innocent or distant anymore. Rather than saying something in response to your question, an adult might try to comfort you instead, without saying a word. The fear in the eyes of the adults intensified your own and made you realize that they too were scared, and might be asking themselves the same questions. You might have been told that people hunt and kill animals for meat and that God made it so, but for the first time you realized that people killed people, too. I had been terrified of pigs and monkeys, but never had my neighbors frightened me before. I heard one adult say, referring to those who killed, "People have become animals." For a child, this seemed to explain why those people could kill other people: they weren't people anymore, they were just animals. But that answer still left a child puzzled. How could people transform into animals? How could you tell which person was capable of transforming into an animal? And when they became animals, why did they remain in their human form? The fables about creatures that were part human and part animal could not explain this either. It was easy to imagine a killer with human legs and arms, but only if it also had a monkey's tail and a pig's head. What the adult meant, I realized, was that people became animals on the inside. I could not see in there. All I could conclude was that the inside of a person was a mystery.

When the war began, I ceased asking questions and became very quiet. At that age, I was just starting to explore the world outside my house and was eager for my parents to let me go play with other kids my age, but I never had that chance. It wasn't so much that war made it too dangerous to play. I didn't feel like a child anymore. I no longer felt like playing. So I skipped a stage in life, and I think it is that missing stage that has left me feeling like a stranger among people my own age.

During the thirteen years of war, evenings were no longer story times but times of terror. When war finally ended, the whole tradition of storytelling was gone. I remember the times of stories with both fondness and sorrow. For me those were joyful times, during which I began to learn about meanings and reasons for things in life, and to make sense of the world within and around myself. The most pleasant times I remember from my childhood are the times of stories. For my country, it was a loss. Storytelling had played an important role in passing on cultural knowledge and collective memory. My hope since I began to write has been to carry on the tradition in my own small way, and to honor my elders and their stories of what used to be.

Acknowledgments

I went through a difficult time writing this book, but I have had the privilege of a wide circle of family and friends, and I am grateful to each one of them; the list would be too long. I am especially grateful to Frances and Tracy Kidder for their invaluable support, and to Maman Clémence and my brother Asvelt, to whom I dedicate this book. Maman Clémence did not live to see it, but she was the light in my life and is the central character of my book, and I hope that this book will keep her flame burning. I am also grateful to my editors at Random House, Kate Medina and Noa Shapiro, for restructuring my book and giving it a new life. This book required a lot of research, and I am grateful to the Whiting Foundation for providing me with a generous grant to complete my research and writing.

I would not have been able to complete this book without Tracy Kidder's mentorship and Kate Medina's relentless support. When I lost my way, they were there to guide me to the shore.

I am also grateful to my former professor, Laurie Heatherington; to my former editor, Anna Pitoniak; and to my literary agent, Wendy Strothman. I also want to thank the people at Random House who have worked on my book and made it possible to bring it into the world. I'm very grateful to my publishers, Gina Centrello (president and publisher of Random House), Andy Ward (publisher of Random House), and Avideh Bashirrad (deputy publisher), and to the production team, Benjamin Dreyer, Rebecca Berlant, Evan Camfield, Victoria Wong, and Mark Maguire. I am also grateful to Carlos Beltran for the jacket design, to Maria Braeckel and Susan Corcoran for publicity, and to Barbara Fillon for marketing.

Bibliographical Note

For too long, in Burundi as in Rwanda, history has been used as a weapon. Some of the works cited here are remarkably tendentious. I have included them because I think it important to consider all points of view when attempting to understand something as complex as a nation's history.

The richest material that I know on Burundian culture and the Bashingantahe was written in Kirundi and French by Burundians, and these works are cited in the bibliography below. When I described Burundian culture in this book, I used the term "ancient" to reflect the fact that the civilization of the region is perhaps the oldest on earth. When Jean Pierre Chrétien writes about precolonial history, he uses the term "ancient Burundi," and he cites archaeological evidence to suggest that settlement in Burundi dates back to at least the first millennium B.C.E.

As I was doing my research, I came across some misinformation about Watusi cattle, also known as the Cattle of Kings. I have cited a couple of websites claiming that the Watusi originated either in Egypt or in India. These websites liken Watusi to the Zebu cattle in Madagascar. These sites are not trustworthy sources, in my view. According to more scholarly works, a combination of genetic studies and archaeological research, including cultural history, indicates that Watusi cattle originated in East Africa. I have also cited several books and articles, and these include *La Civilisation Ancienne des Peuples des Grands Lacs, Imigenzo y'Ikirundi, Cattle of the Ages, Sightings of the Sacred.* The Zebu in Madagascar did come from India, but anyone who has lived among Watusi, as I did, knows that they are utterly different. For instance, their horns can reach a span of ten feet from tip to tip. See "The Saga of the Watusi Cattle."

Some academics suggest that Germans relied exclusively on ruling Burundi through Tutsi chiefs. This is only partly true. The Germans also relied heavily on the use of violence. The ruling strategy in Burundi is documented in a book by a German anthropologist named Hans Meyer, who was in Burundi during the

German occupation (*Die Barundi*). Other scholarly sources include Roger Botte, Jean-Pierre Chrétien, and Burundian historians—Emile Mworoha and Joseph Gahama.

Finally, I want to thank the many people who led me to important documents I could never have found by myself. Given the current political situation in Burundi, I feel obliged *not* to name them for fear of putting them in danger.

Sources

Bigirumwami, Joseph, et al. *L'institution des Bashinga-ntahe au Burundi: Étude pluridisciplinaire*. Bujumbura: Impression INABU, 1999.

Botte, Roger. "Rwanda and Burundi, 1889–1930: Chronology of a Slow Assassination," parts I and II. *International Journal of African Historical Studies* 18, no. 1 (1985): 53–91, and no. 2 (1985): 289–314.

Bukuru, Zacharie. *Les quarante jeunes martyrs de Buta (Burundi 1997): Frères à la vie, à la mort*. Paris: Editions Karthala, 2004.

Burundi 1850–1962. Dir. Ngabo, Léonce. Productions Grands Lacs, 2010.

Camus, Albert. *L'homme révolté*. Paris: Editions Gallimard, 1951.

Centre de Civilisation Burundaise. *La civilisation ancienne des peuples des Grands Lacs*. Bujumbura: C.C.B., 1981.

Chrétien, Jean-Pierre. "Burundi: The Obsession with Genocide." *Current History* 95, no. 601 (May 1996).

————. *The Great Lakes of Africa: Two Thousand Years of History*. Trans. Scott Strauss. New York: Zone Books, 2003.

————. *La crise d'Août 1988 au Burundi*. Paris: Editions AFERA. Diffusion Karthala, 1988.

Chrétien, Jean-Pierre, and Jean-François Dupaquier. *Burundi 1972: Au bord des génocides*. Paris: Editions Karthala, 2007.

Commission internationale d'enquête sur les violations des droits de l'homme au Burundi depuis le 21 octobre 1993. Rapport Final, July 1994.

Dallaire, Roméo. *Shake Hands with the Devil: The Failure of Humanity in Rwanda*. New York: Carroll & Graf, 2003.

Deslaurier, Christine. "Le 'bushingantahe' peut-il réconcilier le Burundi?" *Politique africaine* 4 (2003): 76–96.

Eggers, Ellen K. *Historical Dictionary of Burundi*. 3rd ed. Lanham, Md.: Scarecrow Press, 2006.

Forsythe, David P. *The Humanitarians: The International Committee of the Red Cross*. Cambridge: Cambridge University Press, 2005.

Gahama, Joseph. *Le Burundi sous administration belge*. Paris: Editions Karthala, 1990.

Gourevitch, Philip. *We Wish to Inform You That Tomorrow We Will Be Killed with Our Families*. New York: Farrar, Straus and Giroux, 1998.

Harroy, Jean-Paul. *Burundi 1955–1962. Souvenirs d'un combattant d'une guerre perdue*. Brussels: Hayez, 1987.

Hochschild, Adam. *King Leopold's Ghost: A Story of*

Greed, Terror, and Heroism in Colonial Africa. Boston: Houghton Mifflin, 1998.

Human Rights Watch/Africa Watch, Ligue des Droits de la Personne dans la Region des Grands Lacs, Centre National pour la Coopération au Developpement, Fédération Internationale des Droits de L'Homme, Organisation Mondiale Contre la Torture, National-aal Centrum Voor Ontwikkelingssamenwerking, and NOVIB.

Irankunda, Pacifique, and Laurie Heatherington. "Mental health treatment outcome expectancies in Burundi." *Journal of Transcultural Psychiatry* 54 (2017): 46–65.

Irankunda, Pacifique, et al. "Local Terms and Understandings of Mental Health Problems in Burundi." *Journal of Transcultural Psychiatry* 54 (2017): 66–85.

Kinzer, Stephen. *A Thousand Hills: Rwanda's Rebirth and the Man Who Dreamed It.* Hoboken, N.J.: John Wiley & Sons, 2008.

Krueger, Robert, and Kathleen Tobin Krueger. *From Bloodshed to Hope in Burundi: Our Embassy Years during Genocide.* Austin: University of Texas Press, 2007.

Kubandwa. Dir. Ngabo, Léonce. Productions Grands Lacs, 2010.

Lemarchand, René. *Rwanda and Burundi.* New York: Praeger, 1970.

———. *Burundi: Ethnic Conflict and Genocide.* New York: Woodrow Wilson Center Press, 1996.

Lundgren, Elizabeth. Ankole Watusi International Registry. 16 March 2019. awir.org.

Mamdani, Mahmood. *When Victims Become Killers: Co-*

lonialism, Nativism, and the Genocide in Rwanda. Princeton, N.J.: Princeton University Press, 2001.

———. *Citizen and Subject: Contemporary Africa and the Legacy of Late Colonialism.* Princeton, N.J.: Princeton University Press, 1996.

Manirakiza, Marc. *La fin de la monarchie burundaise (1962–1966).* Brussels: Le Mât de Misaine, 1990.

———. *Burundi: De la révolution au régionalisme, 1966–1976.* Brussels: Le Mât de Misaine, 1992.

———. *Quand le passé ne passe pas (Buyoya I-Ndadaye) 1987–1993.* Brussels: La Longue Vue, 2002.

———. *Les écoles du crime (1994–2005/2006).* Brussels: Le Roseau Vert, 2007.

Mayugi, Nicholas. *La mémoire vigilante et l'interethnique résistante pour une lutte rigoureuse contre le génocide.* Bujumbura: Presses Lavigerie, 1998.

Mbonimpa, Melchior. *Mvukiye Leopold, prête guérisseur: L'aventure du centre de médicine traditionnelle de Buta.* Bujumbura: Les Presses Lavigerie, 2006.

Meyer, Hans. *Die Barundi.* Trans. Will-Mann. Leipzig: Voigtländer, 1916.

Mworoha, Emile. *Histoire du Burundi. Des origines à la fin du XIXème siècle.* Paris: Hatier, 1987.

———. *Peuples et rois de l'Afrique des Lacs: Le Burundi et les royaumes voisins au XIXème siècle.* Dakar-Abidjan: Les Nouvelles Editions Africaines, 1977.

Naudé, Daniel. *Sightings of the Sacred.* New York: Prestel Verlag, 2016.

Newbury, David. *The Land Beyond the Mists: Essays on Identity and Authority in Precolonial Congo and Rwanda.* Athens: Ohio University Press, 2009.

Nibimenya, Albert. *Le nationalisme burundais et ses contradictions: Un état plus nationaliste que national 1961–1988*. Bujumbura: Librairie des lettres et des sciences sociales, 2009.

Nicayenzi, Zénon. *Le Développement durable de l'economie burundaise: Aide-toi, le nord t'aidera*. Bujumbura: Presses Lavigerie, 2006.

Nintunze, Novat. *Burundi 1972: Massacres des Tutsis dans le Sud*. Bujumbura: Editions Iwacu, 2019.

Niyonzima, David, and Lon Fendall. *Ukubanguranya ukurekuriranira no kunywana mu Burundi. Unlocking Horns: Forgiveness and Reconciliation in Burundi*. Newberg, Ore.: Barclay Press, 2001.

Nkanira, Philbert, et al. *Dusome: Igitabu c'umwaka wa gatatu*. Bujumbura: B.E.R., 1993.

Nkeshimana, Germain-Herman. *Mon témoignage: Ce qui n'est pas dit n'existe pas*. Bujumbura: Presses Lavigerie, 2007.

Ntabahungu, Josée, and Marc Manirakiza. *La gloire d'une école (Astrida 1929–1963): Groupe Scolaire d'Astrida*. Bujumbura: Presses de l'IMOBU, 2009.

Ntabona, Adrien. *Les bashingantahe à l'heure de l'interculturation*. Bujumbura: Presses Lavigerie, 2010.

———. *Itinéraire de l'éducation en famille au Burundi: Une approche interculturatrice et complémentariste*. Bujumbura: Presses Lavigerie, 2009.

Ntahokaja, Jean Baptiste. *Imigenzo Y'ikirundi*. Bujumbura: Presses Lavigerie, 1978.

Nyamushirwa, Lydwine. *Iwacu I Burundi. Ijambo mu Ntambwe Z'ubuzima bw'Umurundi*. Bujumbura: Maquette et Impression, 2005.

Prunier, Gerard. "Burundi: A Manageable Crisis?" London: WRITENET (UK), October 1994.

———. "The Great Lakes Crisis." *Current History* 96, no. 610 (May 1997).

Robinson, Michael. *The Lost White Tribe.* New York: Oxford University Press, 2016.

Rodegem, F. M. *Sagesse Kirundi: Proverbes, dictons, locutions usités au Burundi. Annales du Musée Royal du Congo Belge* 34, no. 8. Tervuren, Belgium, 1961.

Rwagasore: Vie, Combat, Espoir. Dir. Justine Bitagoye and Pascal Capitolin. Production La Beneveloncija, 2012, DVD.

Suguru, Sylvère. "La possession par les baganza et son traitement traditionnel." Diss. Université Catholique de Louvain, 1988.

Sweeney, Brittany. The Livestock Conservancy. 2018. 19 Feb 2021. livestockconservancy.org/index.php/heritage /internal/ankole-watusi.

Thibon, Christian. *Histoire démographique du Burundi.* Paris: Editions Karthala, 2004.

Uvin, Peter. *Aiding Violence: The Development Enterprise in Rwanda.* West Hartford, Conn.: Kumarian Press, 1998.

———. "Ethnicity and Power in Burundi and Rwanda: Different Paths to Mass Violence." *Comparative Politics* 35, no. 2 (April 1999).

———. "On Counting and Categorizing the Poor: Census and Power in Burundi and Rwanda." In *Categorizing Citizens: The Use of Race, Ethnicity and Language in National Censuses,* ed. David Kertzer and Dominique Arel. Cambridge: Cambridge University Press, 2001.

————. *Life after Violence: A People's Story of Burundi.* London: Zed Books, 2008.

————. "Structural Causes, Development Cooperation and Conflict Prevention in Burundi and Rwanda." Paper commissioned by and presented at Wilton Park Conference 889—Conflict Prevention and Development in Africa: A Policy Workshop, November 2008. wiltonpark .org.uk/documents/conferences/WP889/participants /participants.aspx.

Vansina, Jan. *La légende du passé: Traditions orales du Burundi.* Musée Royal de l'Afrique Centrale, *Archives d'Anthropologie* 16. Tervuren, Belgium, 1972.

Watt, Nigel. *Burundi, Biography of a Small African Country.* New York: Columbia University Press, 2008.

Weissman, Stephen R. *Preventing Genocide in Burundi: Lessons from International Diplomacy.* Peaceworks 22. Washington, D.C.: United States Institute of Peace, July 1998.

World Watusi Association. "The Cattle of Kings Surface in America." Reprinted from *Watusi World,* winter 1985. watusi.org/2012/05/17/the-cattle-of-kings-surface-in -america.

————. "The Saga of the Watusi Cattle." April 2, 1987. watusi.org/1987/04/02/the-saga-of-the-watusi-cattle.

ABOUT THE AUTHOR

PACIFIQUE IRANKUNDA was born in Burundi, a small country in East Africa bordered by Rwanda, Tanzania, and Congo. He came to America at the age of nineteen as a scholarship student at Deerfield Academy in western Massachusetts. His first published work, "Playing at Violence," appeared in *The American Scholar* and won a Pushcart Prize. He graduated from Williams College with a degree in psychology and political science. He lives in Brooklyn.

This book was set in Sabon, a typeface designed by the well-known German typographer Jan Tschichold (1902–74). Sabon's design is based upon the original letter forms of sixteenth-century French type designer Claude Garamond and was created specifically to be used for three sources: foundry type for hand composition, Linotype, and Monotype. Tschichold named his typeface for the famous Frankfurt typefounder Jacques Sabon (c. 1520–80).